CONVERSATIONS WITH
JEHOVAH'S WITNESSES

RON RHODES

HARVEST HOUSE PUBLISHERS
EUGENE, OREGON

Cover by Dugan Design Group, Bloomington, Minnesota

Cover photo © Design Pics / Don Hammond / Getty Images

CONVERSATIONS WITH JEHOVAH'S WITNESSES
Copyright © 2014 by Ron Rhodes
Published by Harvest House Publishers
Eugene, Oregon 97402
www.harvesthousepublishers.com

Library of Congress Cataloging-in-Publication Data
Rhodes, Ron.
Conversations with Jehovah's Witnesses / Ron Rhodes.
    pages cm
Includes bibliographical references.
ISBN 978-0-7369-5142-5 (pbk.)
ISBN 978-0-7369-5143-2 (eBook)
1. Jehovah's Witnesses—Controversial literature. 2. Witness bearing (Christianity)
3. Apologetics. I. Title.
BX8526.5.R555 2014
289.9'2—'dc23

                                                    2013015296

Printed in the United States of America

        13 14 15 16 17 18 19 20 21 22 / VP-CD / 10 9 8 7 6 5 4 3 2 1

To my beloved wife, Kerri

Acknowledgments

Few books are solo efforts. Most books involve a lot of effort not only from the authors but also from countless other individuals. In different ways, an author's work is impacted by his interactions with his family, friends, professional colleagues, readers, and of course, the publisher with its multiple departments. The more books I write, the more I sense my indebtedness to countless individuals in all these areas and more.

Space constraints allow me to single out only a few. I remain forever thankful for my family—my wife, Kerri, and my two grown children, David and Kylie. I continue to be grateful to the fine folks at Harvest House Publishers—all committed Christians who are true professionals at what they do. Most of all, I express profound thanks and appreciation to our Lord Jesus Christ. What an honor it is to serve Him through the written word.

Contents

Introduction:

Why Another Book on Jehovah's Witnesses?

———— ∞∞∞ ————

Thank you for your interest in this book!

You may be aware that I have already written some books on the Jehovah's Witnesses. The first book I wrote on the subject was *Reasoning from the Scriptures with the Jehovah's Witnesses*, weighing in at a whopping 464 pages. I later wrote a shorter treatment titled *The 10 Most Important Things You Can Say to a Jehovah's Witness*. This slimmed-down book is just 128 pages. For those who want the bottom line, I wrote a 16-page quick reference guide entitled *Jehovah's Witnesses: What You Need to Know*.

I'm grinning a bit as I write. The truth is, Ecclesiastes 12:12 just popped into my mind. This verse says, "Of making many books there is no end, and much study is a weariness of the flesh." So why on earth am I writing yet another book on the Jehovah's Witnesses? Please believe me when I tell you that my goal is not to exhaust your body! To the contrary, my goal is to actually make things easier for you as you continue to be a faithful missionary on your own doorstep when Jehovah's Witnesses visit you.

If you have read one or more of my earlier books on the subject, you will quickly see that this book is not intended to replace the earlier books, but to complement them. Here is the way I look at it.

- *Reasoning from the Scriptures with the Jehovah's Witnesses* is a thorough treatment of what Jehovah's Witnesses believe. It demonstrates precisely why their doctrines are wrong when measured against the Bible. I examine all the primary verses they cite to support their positions. I also include hundreds of questions you can ask to make your points and to start good conversations.

• *The 10 Most Important Things You Can Say to a Jehovah's Witness* provides a concise overview of their beliefs. It focuses on ten primary points you can make during dialogue.

• The quick-reference guide, *Jehovah's Witnesses: What You Need to Know*, contains a brief 16-page listing of their primary doctrinal problems and the appropriate biblical responses.

• The present book demonstrates how to actually engage Jehovah's Witnesses in effective dialogue. It will show you the right way to do it.

The sample conversations in this book contain the verses that are most likely to surface in dialogue with a Jehovah's Witness. Of course, these conversations do not include every possible verse—that would be impossible in a conversation-style, medium-sized book like this. In the interest of covering the most ground while being sensitive to brevity, I have included conversations on representative verses, thereby demonstrating the basics of how to effectively dialogue with Jehovah's Witnesses.

If you desire to go deeper in a particular area, or if you desire full information on all the verses that could come up during dialogue, my comprehensive book *Reasoning from the Scriptures with the Jehovah's Witnesses* will be a big help to you. For your convenience, I have provided page numbers for supplemental reading at the end of each chapter in part 2.

Tactical Conversations

This book is intended to teach you how to engage in tactical conversations with Jehovah's Witnesses that will yield maximum evangelistic punch. *Merriam-Webster's 11th Collegiate Dictionary* offers this as one of the definitions of "tactical": "of or relating to small-scale actions serving a larger purpose." The tactical conversations demonstrated in this book have the larger purpose of helping Jehovah's Witnesses perceive the error of Watchtower theology and become believers in the true God, the true Jesus, and the true gospel.

When I was a teenager, many of my friends and I took a driving class at my high school. The teacher began by explaining the basics of how to operate cars—how to use the gas pedal, the brakes, the turn signals, the windshield wipers, the emergency flashers, and the like. All of this took place in a classroom setting.

Imagine if the teacher then gave me some car keys, put me in a car, gave me two thumbs up, and said, "Go have a nice drive." I might well have had an accident. This is why driving instructors provide on-the-job training in addition to classroom instruction. My teacher took me out on the road every day for three weeks, personally demonstrating everything I needed to know in order to drive safely. By the end of that time, I was ready to drive on my own.

Learning to cook an omelet is much the same. A person can learn a lot about making omelets by reading a cookbook. But it's far better if an experienced cook demonstrates the exact procedure—showing the novice cook what he or she needs to know about the pan temperature, the right order for introducing each ingredient, how to flip the omelet in the pan, and the like. Personal training makes all the difference!

Not all driving instructors teach the same way, and neither do all chefs. That does not mean one is wrong and the other is right. It simply means that their tactics are different. Both may have merit, and both might yield positive results. Similarly, my method of conversing with Jehovah's Witnesses is not the only method that can yield results. God has blessed the Christian church with many fine apologists, and we can learn much from them. I've listed many of their books in the bibliography. I offer my approach with the hope and prayer that many Jehovah's Witnesses will be delivered from the domain of darkness and find entrance into the kingdom of light (Colossians 1:13).

The Difference Between Teaching and Training

There is a big difference between teaching and training. Christian author Kathi Hudson recounts a story told by her father that I think perfectly illustrates this difference.

Since World War II, I've been a trained commercial pilot with an instrument rating. Because of my good training and extensive experience, I could sit a young, 21-year-old man in a classroom and teach him: FAA and Naval Regulations; navigation; aircraft ordinance; mechanical indoctrination; and radio procedures. He could pass all the examinations just fine. He would have had good conscientious teaching.

However, if I were to put him in a new jet fighter plane, pat him on the helmet and say, "Have a nice flight, son," what would happen? It is likely he would crash and burn before he ever got off the runway. Why? He had good teaching but NO TRAINING.

Training always involves teaching, but teaching seldom includes training. Teaching with actual flight training would have saved the young pilot's life and the $15 million fighter plane. Training would ensure him of a good future in flying…To train this young man, I would take him on flights where I piloted, so I could model proper procedure.[1]

My goal in this book is to both teach and train you to engage in effective conversations with Jehovah's Witnesses. I will provide some on-the-job training by giving examples of conversations with Jehovah's Witnesses. As you eavesdrop on these conversations, you will learn the ins and outs of effective tactical conversations.

Please note that the conversations I include in this book are not real, but they are realistic. They are not actual transcripts of witnessing sessions I have had with Jehovah's Witnesses. (Such would make for choppy reading at best.) But the conversations are realistic in that I deal with many of the actual issues that will most likely come up on your doorstep. I thoroughly demonstrate how to respond to such issues.

Please also note that in each conversation I not only deal with the particular issue they bring up, but I also take every opportunity to show that the Watchtower Society, which claims to be the mouthpiece of Jehovah, is not a trustworthy source of truth. The more successful you are in chipping away at the doctrines of the Watchtower Society in a kind but truthful manner, the more the Jehovah's Witness will be open to hearing what you have to say. This two-pronged approach—exposing errors in the teaching of the Watchtower Society and communicating biblical truth—is extremely effective.

Biblically Based Tactics

I intend to take a biblical approach in this book. I will cite lots of Scripture—not only in the sample conversations, which demonstrate how to refute the false views of the Jehovah's Witnesses, but also when I describe the methods I use to communicate truth to them. Scripture must always be central. I encourage you to be like the Berean Christians of old, who tested the apostle Paul's teachings against Scripture: "They received the word with all eagerness, examining the Scriptures daily to see if these things were so" (Acts 17:11).

Paul himself wrote, "Test everything; hold fast to what is good" (1 Thessalonians 5:21). Bible expositor Thomas Constable says Paul's readers "could do this by comparing what the speaker said with the standard of previously given divine revelation (cf. Deut. 13:1-5; 18:20; 1 John 4:1-3)."[2] Our goal, then, is to test all things against Scripture, which is our sole barometer of truth. By doing this, we can better engage Jehovah's Witnesses in helpful conversations.

You Witness but God Converts

It is important that I remind you of a foundational truth. You and I are called to be witnesses to the truth of the Bible (Matthew 28:19-20; Acts 1:8). We do not have the power in ourselves to convert anyone. That is God's job. You and I witness; only our supernatural and miraculous God has the power to convert (see John 6:39-40,44).

Many Christians throughout church history have noted the miraculous element involved in a fallen sinner converting to Christ. Baptist preacher Adrian Rogers said that "the greatest miracle is the transformation that God works when he regenerates a soul."[3] The German reformer Martin Luther commented, "Conversion is the greatest of all miracles."[4] Henry Morris said that "the miracle of regeneration is a grade A miracle in every sense of the word."[5]

Here is why I bring this up. You and I as God's witnesses can be used as God's instruments to communicate God's transforming truth so that it eventually may lead to God's supernatural conversion of a lost soul (such as a Jehovah's Witness). Knowing that it is God's job to do the converting takes the weight off of you and me in our witnessing encounters. Following our faithful witness, we leave the results with God. If the Jehovah's Witness with whom we are speaking does not convert, we can rest in the comfort of knowing that we have been faithful witnesses and that the results are in God's sovereign hands.

Perhaps a gardening metaphor might help. Some of us plant seeds when we share the gospel. We may be the first to share the true gospel with a particular Jehovah's Witness. Others of us water the seed that has already been planted in the heart of the Jehovah's Witness. We do this by continuing to share the truth of God's Word with him. Others of us, fewer in number, experience the joy of seeing the flower blossom—that is, we are privileged to see him become a true believer in Christ by the power of God.

So don't become discouraged if you don't see an immediate conversion after your dialogue with the Jehovah's Witness. Just focus on being faithful in planting and watering the seed. It is then in God's sovereign hands. As the Christian singer Keith Green once said, "Do your best, pray that it's blessed, and the Lord will take care of the rest."

Charting Our Course

This book is divided into two parts. Part 1 contains seven chapters that deal with the basics of tactical conversing. Here I lay a foundation for you. What you learn in these seven chapters will prove useful in witnessing to Jehovah's Witnesses and anyone else who is not a Christian.

Part 2 builds on part 1 by providing specific insights on conversing with Jehovah's Witnesses on important doctrinal issues, such as God, Jesus, the Holy Spirit, the Trinity, the gospel that saves, and the afterlife. In each chapter, I contrast what Jehovah's Witnesses believe on a particular issue with what the Bible teaches. I point you to specific issues to watch for, and I summarize "Important Points to Introduce." Then I get to the heart of the chapter—"Eavesdropping on a Conversation." I bring up Scripture references that are likely to surface in the conversation. Following sample conversations, I provide some very brief "Conversation Highlights," in which I remind you of key components of my conversation. By using this simple methodology, my goal is to equip you to become a confident missionary on your own doorstep.

There is one more thing. You will notice that at the beginning of each chapter in part 2, I remind you to pray what I call the open-the-heart prayer. No such prayer is actually referenced in the Bible. However, I based my idea on Acts 16:14. According to this verse, a businesswoman named Lydia was listening to the apostle Paul speak, and "the Lord opened her heart to pay attention to what was said by Paul." Every time a Jehovah's Witness rings your doorbell and you begin a conversation, silently pray that the Lord would open his or her heart to pay attention to what you have to say. Remember—only God has the power to convert.

> *Father, I pray that by the power of the Holy Spirit, You will enlighten the understanding of my readers so that they can fully grasp how to most effectively communicate the good news of the gospel to Jehovah's Witnesses. Please remove any fears they may have about witnessing encounters. Grant them Your peace as they share the good news. May our combined efforts lead to many Jehovah's Witnesses becoming believers in the true Messiah, Jesus Christ. Amen.*

PART 1

The Basics of Tactical Conversing

1

Why Effective Conversation Matters

———∞∞∞———

Advice columnist Abigail Van Buren once commented, "In my view, the height of arrogance is to attempt to show people the 'errors' in the religion of their choice."[1] Her thinking implies a commandment—"Thou shalt not infringe upon my religious truth." Of course, if we heeded Van Buren's advice, apologetic conversations with Jehovah's Witnesses (and others) would never take place, and countless souls would enter eternity without having heard the gospel of Jesus Christ.

Tragically, some Christians avoid dialoguing with Jehovah's Witnesses for other reasons. Some are fearful of engaging in such dialogue. Others are too busy with their own plans for the day. Still other Christians rationalize that Jehovah's Witnesses follow the "devil's religion" and should be treated accordingly. Some Christians even slam the door in the face of Jehovah's Witnesses.

The problem with the last of these responses is that it ends up reinforcing, in the minds of Jehovah's Witnesses, their claim to be the true people of God. Just as God's people were mistreated and persecuted in Old and New Testament times, so the Jehovah's Witnesses claim to be the persecuted people of God today. They believe they are modern martyrs in a long line of victims throughout history. Christian apologist Wilbur Lingle reports, "I have been to their Kingdom Halls and heard them sing a song about going from door to door and how people will slam the door in their faces—but they will be 'true to Jehovah because they are receiving persecution for his sake.'"[2]

My best advice is to always be willing to converse with Jehovah's Witnesses whenever they show up on your doorstep, and to do it with kindness and respect (see 1 Peter 3:15-16). Never forget that God will use you as His instrument to reach the lost. This book will help you to be prepared.

A Kingdom Assignment

Throughout biblical history and to this day, God has chosen to reach people through other people. For example, God chose the Jews to be a light for the nations and appointed them to share the good news of God with all other people around the world (see Isaiah 42:6). The Jews were to be God's representatives to the Gentiles. The Jews failed at this task and didn't even recognize Jesus as the divine Messiah. Nevertheless, this was their divine calling.

Among the Jews themselves, the priests were called to represent God to the people and to represent the people to God (Exodus 30:10). God employed the priests as intermediaries to maintain His relationship with the Jewish people.

All the while, the Old Testament prophets were on the scene, often beginning their revelations from God with "Thus says the LORD" (as in Exodus 4:22, for example). They communicated God's revelation to the people as God spoke through them. Then, in New Testament times, God communicated His revelations to people through the apostles (see Acts 4:33).

Today, God calls Christian churches and individual Christians to be His representatives in sharing the good news of the gospel with other people throughout the world (Matthew 28:19-20; Acts 1:8). Just as He did in times past, God today works *through* people in making Himself known *to* people. This has always been His modus operandi.

The relevance of this fact for witnessing to Jehovah's Witnesses is obvious. You and I as Christians are God's representatives, empowered to communicate the truth of Scripture to those we encounter, including Jehovah's Witnesses. Never forget that God reaches people through His own people. For this reason, when Jehovah's Witnesses show up on our doorstep, we can know that God is giving us a kingdom assignment. Do we dare say no?

Goal-Driven Conversations

When conversing with Jehovah's Witnesses, we engage in goal-driven conversation. Our goal is to help them become truly informed about Watchtower theology. We want to provide information that leads them to the true God, the true Jesus, and the true gospel that saves. As one Christian apologist put it, "The ultimate goal of a Christian conversing with a Jehovah's Witness should be to lead him to personal faith in our wonderful Lord and Savior Jesus Christ."[3]

There is a strong precedent in Scripture for using the spoken word to persuade men and women to accept God's truth. The apostle Paul instructed young Timothy about this.

> I charge you in the presence of God and of Christ Jesus, who is to judge the living and the dead, and by his appearing and his kingdom: preach the word; be ready in season and out of season; reprove, rebuke, and exhort, with complete patience and teaching (2 Timothy 4:1-2).

Church leaders are required to "hold firm to the trustworthy word as taught, so that [they] may be able to give instruction in sound doctrine and also to rebuke those who contradict it" (Titus 1:9). Paul himself loved to reason from the Scriptures with people.

> Paul went in, as was his custom, and on three Sabbath days he reasoned with them from the Scriptures, explaining and proving that it was necessary for the Christ to suffer and to rise from the dead, and saying, "This Jesus, whom I proclaim to you, is the Christ." And some of them were persuaded and joined Paul and Silas, as did a great many of the devout Greeks and not a few of the leading women (Acts 17:2-4).

Of course, apostles and church leaders were not the only ones to engage in goal-driven conversations with people. We have seen that you and I, too, are called to be engaged in the evangelistic process.

Always Be Ready with an Answer

First Peter 3:15-16 is foundational to our tactical strategy in witnessing to Jehovah's Witnesses. "Set apart the Messiah as Lord in your hearts, and always be ready to give a defense to anyone who asks you for a reason for the hope that is in you. However, do this with gentleness and respect, keeping your conscience clear" (HCSB). Let's briefly examine the key components of this passage.

Honor the Messiah Jesus as Lord in Your Hearts

Each of us must honor Christ as Lord in our hearts. He is our sovereign Master. When we are in full submission to the lordship of Christ, we think about our conversations with Jehovah's Witnesses in new ways.

- We recognize that Christ is in charge. When witnessing to a Jehovah's Witness, we are fulfilling the Great Commission.

- We recognize that Christ is in charge of the outcome of the conversation. We must not forget that our job is simply to speak about the truth of Scripture and that it is God's job to convert. This takes the burden off of us in witnessing encounters.

- Because Christ is in charge, we need not have any fear about the witnessing encounter (see Psalm 118:6; Hebrews 13:6). As one commentator put it, "To reverence Christ as Lord means to believe that Jesus Christ is in control and that those who come against the believer are not. To have such reverence is to maintain a deep-seated confidence in Jesus Christ as the reigning Lord of the universe."[4] Put another way, "our fear of the Lord should drive out all fear of men."[5] So don't sweat it when you converse with Jehovah's Witnesses. The Lord is with you. Share the truth in peace.

Be Ready to Respond

Do you have an eternal hope that is plainly evident to all those you meet? Or are you more like a secret-agent Christian who has never blown his cover? The truth is, only people who become aware that you have an eternal hope will ask you about it. My exhortation, then, is that we should all be open and free about our hope in Jesus Christ. Especially when Jehovah's Witnesses show up on the doorstep, we ought to speak in such a way that they quickly perceive that we are truly excited about our eternal hope. Don't mask it. Don't camouflage it. Be a shining light— a sparkling diamond—so that they can see that something is different about you (Matthew 5:16). As one Bible scholar put it, "Christian hope is to be so real and distinctive that non-Christians will be puzzled by it and ask for an explanation."[6]

When someone asks us about our eternal hope, we need to be ready with an answer, as 1 Peter 3:15-16 instructs. Bible expositor Thomas Constable says, "We should have the reason we are living as we do on the tip of our tongues so whenever an opportunity arises we can explain why we behave as we do (cf. Acts 22:1; 25:16)."[7]

Once they ask us, we can make our defense. The word "defense" in this verse comes from the Greek word *apologia,* from which we derive the English term "apologetics." In New Testament times the term was often used of a formal legal defense in a court of law (see Acts 25:16; 2 Timothy 4:16).[8] The apostle Paul adapted the term in regard to defending the truth of Christianity (see Philippians 1:16).

Always Use Gentleness and Respect

Peter reminds us to make our defense of the truth with gentleness and respect. These words are rich in meaning. The word "gentleness" carries the idea of meekness and humility. There is not to be even the slightest hint of arrogance (see 1 Peter 3:4). This does not mean that the Christian defender is to seem weak or hesitant, but rather that he or she is to communicate strong truth from the Bible in a gentle and humble way. The Christian should certainly not ram truth down people's throats, speak patronizingly, act condescendingly, or have a critical countenance. Let's not forget that soft answers are the most effective because they "turn away wrath" (Proverbs 15:1). A gentle answer is much easier to swallow.

The word "respect" has two important nuances. On the one hand, we are to maintain a reverential awe of God (see 1 Peter 1:17; 2:17; 3:2). On the other hand, we are to treat Jehovah's Witnesses with respect (see Colossians 4:6).

I urge you to burn the words "gentleness" and "respect" into your heart. Your theological arguments may be strong, but they will have little effect if they are not communicated with gentleness and respect.

We Are Ambassadors of Christ

Perhaps one of the best pictures of a person who communicates with gentleness and respect is an ambassador. The apostle Paul says "we are ambassadors for Christ, God making his appeal through us" (2 Corinthians 5:20). Previously, I noted that God primarily reaches people through people. Here we are told that God reaches the unsaved through you and me as ambassadors of Christ.

Christian apologist Don Closson has some great insights on the ambassador model of witnessing.

> We need fewer frontal assaults and more embassy meetings. The skills necessary to be a successful ambassador are quite different from those of an infantryman. Persuasion rather than conquest motivate the ambassador, and one's style of communication can be as important as the content being conveyed.[9]

It is not just *what* you say that is important, it is also *how* you say it. Gregory Koukl, another Christian apologist, highlights three primary skill sets of an ambassador of Christ.

> First, a Christian ambassador should possess a clear understanding of the message being offered by his sovereign King. Second, he needs to exhibit a personal character that

reinforces the message he's been charged with, not distract from it. Finally, an ambassador needs sufficient wisdom to know how to communicate his message in a manner that draws people into dialogue and then to keep the conversation going.[10]

Showing gentleness and respect are two of the key requisites for drawing people into dialogue and keeping the conversation going. Never forget that the way you and I carry out our task as Christ's ambassadors will determine in large measure how open Jehovah's Witnesses will be to the true Christ and the true gospel. "People will think more highly or less highly of Christ and his church based on the effectiveness of his ambassadors' service."[11]

2

The Importance of Listening

⸻◦⊷◦⸻

Did you know that God's will is for you to be a good listener? James 1:19 instructs, "Let every person be quick to hear, slow to speak, slow to anger." Being a good listener is a key component of effective conversations with Jehovah's Witnesses.

Reflecting on this verse, Bible expositor Alec Motyer commented that "the great talker is rarely a great listener, and never is the ear more firmly closed than when anger takes over."[1] There is a lot of wisdom here. Witnessing to Jehovah's Witnesses does not just involve talking well about biblical truths. One simply cannot engage in effective apologetic conversations with Jehovah's Witnesses without listening to the specifics of what they are saying. And we must take special care to listen without even a hint of anger arising either in our voice or our countenance. Maintaining composure can be a challenge when they express heresies about Jesus. But I encourage you to let the love of Jesus shine through your face even as they promote error.

I feel compelled to warn you that Satan may tempt you to show anger, for he knows that if you do, you will likely forfeit your evangelistic success. Beware of the tactics of the devil (see Ephesians 6:11). One Bible scholar warns, "The restraint of anger is demanded, for anger closes the mind to God's truth. A fiercely argumentative attitude is not conducive to the humble reception of truth."[2]

Another key verse about the importance of listening well is Proverbs 18:13: "If one gives an answer before he hears, it is his folly and shame." It is foolish for people to "blurt out opinions on matters that they have not taken the trouble to hear carefully. One should listen well before speaking."[3]

Some Christians may feel that if they do not interrupt the Jehovah's Witnesses' falsehoods, they are consenting to what is being shared. But that is not true. Christian apologist Charles Strohmer offers this wise advice:

> Some Christians get tripped up because they assume that to listen and to understand is to agree, and they don't want to be complicit with false beliefs...You do not have to like what you're hearing. The purpose is to understand the person so that at a later point...Christ can be shared. Understanding is a prerequisite to persuasion.[4]

So let Jehovah's Witnesses speak unhindered for a few minutes. You will have the opportunity to respond soon enough. As they share their heresies, don't roll your eyes, clench your teeth, cross your arms, make a fist, cluck your tongue, furrow your brow, breathe out loud and rapid exhales, or engage in any other theatrics. Just keep a pleasant look on your face and let them speak. Your patient listening will pay off.

Listening Shows Interest and Care

Listening demonstrates to people that you care about them and are interested in them. It shows that your verbal engagement with them is not just a dialectic contest to see who wins. It demonstrates that they are so important to you personally that you will give your time to hear them out.

Keep in mind that Jehovah's Witnesses expect to be interrupted. They have been taught that they are God's persecuted martyrs. When you interrupt, you reinforce these beliefs, so surprise them by hearing them out. Surprise them with kindness. Listening well keeps you from focusing on an opposing position and helps you to see a real person.[5] You will also find that the more effectively you listen to what they say, the more their defenses will come down. Norman and David Geisler, in their book *Conversational Evangelism*, suggest that "if people sense you are genuinely trying to understand them, they may be less defensive and let down their guard to engage in honest dialogue."[6]

During the witnessing encounter, be sure to remember their names.

Ask about their families. Learn as much as you can about their personal lives—their vocations, their hobbies, and their likes and dislikes. After they leave, jot down a few notes so that the next time they visit, you can greet them by name, inquire about their family members by name, and ask how their hobbies are going. Nothing says "I care" as much as remembering personal details. You will find that this will contribute greatly to building a personal relationship with them. Christian apologist Wilbur Lingle suggests beginning and ending your times of conversation on a personal note.[7] This will keep that personal relationship growing with each visit. And the more your personal relationship grows, the more they will listen to you when you bring up problems about Watchtower theology.

Listening with Focused Attention

We all occasionally pretend to listen when we are really not listening at all. Sometimes we think about all the other stuff we need to do. Sometimes we daydream. Sometimes we get distracted. Sometimes, for whatever reason, we just space out. When dialoguing with Jehovah's Witnesses, be careful to give them your focused attention. Think about how you would feel if you were explaining what you believe to someone, only to discover that he wasn't even listening. You wouldn't like it. Show others the courtesy of your full attention.

Listening Without Interruption

Do you remember the last time you got into an argument with someone? Did you interrupt her when she was speaking? You probably did. We all do it.

The temptation to do this in religious discussions is especially strong. After all, we take our religious views very seriously. You and I love God. We love Jesus Christ. We are profoundly grateful for the gospel of grace, the only true gospel of salvation. When people show up on our doorsteps and begin speaking untruths about God, Jesus, and the gospel, our first inclination is to stop them dead in their tracks and launch into a preemptive defense of the truth.

Been there, done that. This is exactly what I did as a young Christian many years ago. I had zeal without knowledge. I wanted to defend the truth. In those early years, I had no idea that by constantly interrupting Jehovah's Witnesses by saying, "That's wrong," "That's nonsense," or "No way is that true," I was being offensive and inadvertently erecting a barrier between us. My tactic was sincere but misguided. The truth is, they *were* wrong. They did spew out nonsense, and what they said was in no way true. But my relentless interruptions were a huge turnoff for them.

My friends, resist the temptation. Do not interrupt. Be patient and let them speak without interruption. Let them finish whatever point they are making, and then you can calmly respond with a pleasant look on your face.

Listening Helps You Understand

Too often we as Christians have a tendency to tell cultists what they believe. This is not wise. I can say from long experience that when you tell Jehovah's Witnesses what they believe, they are likely to say, "Well, I don't believe that." It is much better to listen to what they say so you can hear from their own mouths what they believe. As Norman and David Geisler put it, "To be more effective in reaching others, we will have to work harder on really listening to people to know what they believe so we can know better how to reach them. Everything begins with careful listening."[8]

One of the best ways to show Jehovah's Witnesses that you have been listening is to restate what they said. You might say something like, "Okay, let me make sure I understand you correctly. You believe that..." Then, after you have restated their view, ask them if you have understood them correctly. The benefit of this approach is twofold. It proves that you have given them an attentive ear, and it clearly delineates their position so that you will be able to properly and accurately respond from the Bible.

Beware of the Terminology Block

Cults such as the Jehovah's Witnesses typically use Christian doctrinal words, such as God, Jesus, atonement, salvation, resurrection, and second coming, but they pour their own cultic meanings into those words. For example, consider this statement: Jesus Christ is God, was crucified and died, and was resurrected from the dead.

You and I can agree with that statement. Jehovah's Witnesses would too. But here is how they would hear it:

• Jesus is a mighty god who is lesser than the Father.

• Jesus was crucified on a stake, not a cross.

• Jesus was resurrected spiritually, not physically.

Such redefinitions should not surprise us, for Scripture itself cautions us in this regard. Second Corinthians 11:4, for example, warns us of a different Jesus, a different spirit, and a different gospel (see also Matthew 24:24; Acts 20:28-31; Galatians 1:6-9; 2 Peter 2:1-3).

The importance of recognizing the terminology block cannot be overstated. As my friend Walter Martin once put it, "Unless terms are defined when one is either speaking or reading cult theology, the semantic jungle that the cults have created will envelop him, making difficult, if not impossible, a proper contrast between the teachings of the cults and those of orthodox Christianity."[9]

Listen with a View to Apologetic Response

As we listen to the Jehovah's Witnesses, we listen *strategically.* That is, we are listening for discrepancies in their viewpoint, logical fallacies, points of disagreement with the Bible, false caricatures of true Christianity, and the like. As they speak, we can make a mental note of each item that calls for an apologetic response.

To illustrate, one Jehovah's Witness I was speaking to was addressing my question about one of the false prophecies of the Watchtower Society. The Watchtower had prophesied that in 1925, Abraham, Isaac, Jacob, and other Old Testament patriarchs would be resurrected from the dead and would live in a mansion in San Diego called Beth Sarim. (It didn't happen.) He replied that the "light" is much brighter today and that Jehovah's Witnesses consequently have much better prophetic insight today than they did earlier.

As he was speaking, I listened without interruption and with atten-tiveness. I was very kind. At the same time, I was listening strategically. I was watching for flaws in his thinking. When he finished speaking, I said something like this: "Thanks for explaining that. But may I ask you a question? What if thirty years from now there is so much new light that you discover that everything you believe today is wrong? And also, what if you die tomorrow? Will you go into eternity having believed error?"

That question got his attention. The point I am making, of course, is that the more strategically we listen, the better our apologetic responses will be.

To sum up, good defenders of the faith are good listeners. Good lis-teners shape their comments to fit the exact comments of the people with whom they are speaking. If we do not listen well, our follow-up questions will be off base and irrelevant.

We'll look at the use of questions in the next chapter.

3

The Importance of Asking Questions

———∞———

Our God is a God of reason (Isaiah 1:18). He has constructed us to be rational creatures in His own image (Genesis 1:27; Colossians 3:10), so reason necessarily plays a role in all our deliberations.

The Bible is filled with exhortations to use reason. Jesus commanded His followers, "Love the Lord your God...with all your mind" (Matthew 22:37). The apostle Paul added, "Whatever is true...think about these things" (Philippians 4:8). We are told that Paul "reasoned in the synagogue with the Jews" (Acts 17:17) as he did with philosophers in the Areopagus (verses 22-31). Church elders are instructed to refute those who contradict sound doctrine (Titus 1:9). Paul says he was appointed for "the defense of the gospel" (Philippians 1:16). Jude urged, "Contend for the faith that was once for all delivered to the saints" (Jude 3). We have seen that Peter commanded us, "[Be] prepared to make a defense to anyone who asks you for a reason for the hope that is in you" (1 Peter 3:15). All these activities involve the use of God-given reason.

You and I were designed by a God of reason to be people who reason. It is a part of our nature. So it makes sense that the use of reasonable questions can play a significant role in conversations with Jehovah's Witnesses.

I can say from long experience that when talking to Jehovah's Witnesses, we will never be successful forcing our opinions or our theology down their throats. On the other hand, helping a Jehovah's Witness to discover problems in Watchtower theology for himself is possible—and much more helpful.

Here's one way to help a Jehovah's Witness discover problems in

Watchtower theology—ask strategic questions based on key verses, all the while remaining tactful and kind. Jesus often asked questions to make a point. As Christian apologist David Reed notes, "Rather than shower his listeners with information, [Jesus] used questions to draw answers out of them. A person can close his ears to facts he doesn't want to hear, but if a pointed question causes him to form the answer in his own mind, he cannot escape the conclusion—because it's a conclusion that he reached himself."[1] Indeed, "asking questions can prove to be more effective than all the right and irrefutable arguments we can muster."[2]

Here is a brief sampling of Bible passages that illustrate how Jesus asked questions to make a point or to draw a response out of His hearers.

- "As he was setting out on his journey, a man ran up and knelt before him and asked him, 'Good Teacher, what must I do to inherit eternal life?' And Jesus said to him, 'Why do you call me good? No one is good except God alone'" (Mark 10:17-18). Jesus used this question to help the man see that by calling Him good, he was ultimately calling Him God.

- The Pharisees, seeking to trap Jesus, said to Him, "'Tell us, then, what you think. Is it lawful to pay taxes to Caesar, or not?' But Jesus, aware of their malice, said, 'Why put me to the test, you hypocrites? Show me the coin for the tax.' And they brought him a denarius. And Jesus said to them, 'Whose likeness and inscription is this?' They said, 'Caesar's.' Then he said to them, 'Therefore render to Caesar the things that are Caesar's, and to God the things that are God's'" (Matthew 22:17-21).

- "[Jesus] went on from there and entered their synagogue. And a man was there with a withered hand. And they [the Pharisees] asked him, 'Is it lawful to heal on the Sabbath?'—so that they might accuse him. He said to them, 'Which one of you who has a sheep, if it falls into a pit on the Sabbath, will not take hold of it and lift it out? Of how much more value is a man than a sheep! So it is lawful to do good on the Sabbath'" (Matthew 12:9-12).

- "When Jesus came into the district of Caesarea Philippi, he asked his disciples, 'Who do people say that the Son of Man is?' And they said, 'Some say John the Baptist, others say Elijah, and others Jeremiah or one of the prophets.' He said to them, 'But who do you say that I am?' Simon Peter replied, 'You are the Christ, the Son of the living God'" (Matthew 16:13-16).

Norman and David Geisler note that "the Gospels record over 200 questions that Jesus asked. He was a master at asking questions."[3] In each case, Jesus used the question to effectively make a point. We must use this same type of methodology with Jehovah's Witnesses. The right question asked in a nondefensive, unchallenging, unemotional way might cause the Jehovah's Witness to find himself face-to-face with a doctrine—the absolute deity of Christ, for example—that is completely contrary to what the Watchtower Society has taught him. By considering such a question, the Jehovah's Witness is forced to come to a conclusion in his own mind.

So, for example, you might begin by asking the Jehovah's Witness how many true Gods there are, according to John 17:3. Allow him to open his New World Translation and read it aloud. "This means everlasting life, their taking in knowledge of you, the only true God, and of the one whom you sent forth, Jesus Christ." Based on this verse, the Jehovah's Witness will say that Jehovah (the Father) is the one true God.

Next, point out that according to John 1:1 in the New World Translation, Jesus is "a god." Ask the Jehovah's Witness if he agrees that Jesus is "a god." The answer will be yes. Then ask whether Jesus is a true god or a false god. This will cause a dilemma for the Jehovah's Witness. If he says Jesus is a false god, he is contradicting the New World Translation of Scripture (since John 1:1 in this version says Jesus is a god). If he says Jesus is a true god, he is also contradicting the Watchtower understanding of Scripture, for John 17:3 says there is only one true God—Jehovah.

I think you can see what I mean when I say that a well-placed question can be a lot more effective than assaulting a Jehovah's Witness with your proof of the deity of Christ (or any other doctrine). If you and the Jehovah's Witness agree to meet every week or two to discuss different issues, you can rest assured that the cumulative effect of such questions will slowly but surely erode his belief system so that he is more open to the true gospel.

I wrote *Reasoning from the Scriptures with the Jehovah's Witnesses* more than two decades ago. In that book, I espoused a strategy of asking questions to both clarify beliefs and to make important theological points. Since that time, a number of very helpful apologetics books have been published that also recognize the importance of asking well-placed questions. These include *Conversational Evangelism* by Norman and David Geisler, *Tactics: A Game Plan for Discussing Your Christian Convictions* by Gregory Koukl, and *Approaching Jehovah's Witnesses in Love* by Wilbur Lingle. I highly recommend these books and will highlight a few important points from them.

In recent years, David Geisler, Gregory Koukl, and others have called this question-asking strategy the "Columbo tactic," named after the TV detective, Lieutenant Columbo.* Koukl says, "The key to the Columbo tactic is to go on the offensive in an inoffensive way by using carefully selected questions to productively advance the conversation. Simply put, never make a statement, at least at first, when a question will do the job."[4] I wholeheartedly agree!

Koukl goes on to describe three kinds of questions one can ask in using the Columbo tactic. Norman and David Geisler address these same kinds of questions, as do I in my *Reasoning from the Scriptures with the Jehovah's Witnesses*.

- Ask questions to gather information. That is, ask questions to find out what the person actually believes.
- Ask questions to put the burden of proof on the person.

---

* I was privileged to spend a day with actor Peter Falk, who played Lieutenant Columbo on the popular series, in Hollywood back in the 1970s. I have a special affection for Columbo!

That is, ask questions to make the Jehovah's Witness prove that his view is correct.

- Ask questions to move the conversation in a specific direction. For example, ask questions designed to help the Jehovah's Witness recognize that the doctrine of the Trinity is true.[5]

Let's examine these categories of questions in a bit more detail.

Fact-Gathering Questions

During the early stage of your conversation with Jehovah's Witnesses, ask questions for the purpose of gathering facts. Such questions can help you ascertain and clarify what they believe.

If Jehovah's Witnesses show up unexpectedly and you are not quite sure what to say initially, you can easily and immediately ask fact-gathering questions about what they believe. By asking such questions, you immediately shift the discussion back onto their shoulders, thereby buying yourself more time to consider a response.

As they tell you what they believe, you can clarify their beliefs by asking, "So, let me make sure I understand you. Are you saying that...?" And then you can ask, "Have I understood you correctly?" Christian apologist Don Closson notes, "Good questions protect us from jumping to conclusions" and help us to "deal with the actual beliefs a person holds rather than some straw man position that we might prefer to attack."[6]

Asking fact-gathering questions is important, for not every Jehovah's Witness believes the same as others. I remember talking to two Jehovah's Witness ladies on the doorstep. One was a Jehovah's Witness trainer, and the other was an apprentice. After listening to the trainer for a few minutes, I asked, "So, let me make sure I understand you. You believe in two different gods. One is a God Almighty, and the other is a lesser god. Is that right?" The apprentice immediately shook her head side to side and said with passion, "Oh no, we don't believe that." The trainer then nodded up and down, and said, "Yeah, we believe that." (It was actually quite hilarious, though I chose to restrain my laughter.)

The apprentice—with eyes wide as pancakes—attempted to maintain her cool. In any event, by asking clarifying questions, I was able to narrow down exactly what these ladies believed, or at least what one of them believed.

Fact-gathering questions will also inform you of the specific things you will need to respond to from an apologetic perspective.

Questions That Shift the Burden of Proof

Some questions are engineered to gather facts, but others are intended to put the burden of proof on the other person. These questions are asked to force Jehovah's Witnesses to prove that their view is correct, as opposed to the view espoused by traditional historic Christianity. Koukl says, "The burden of proof is the responsibility someone has to defend or give evidence for his view...Whoever makes the claim bears the burden."[7]

With this in mind, our goal at this early juncture in our witnessing encounter is not to prove that the view of historic Christianity is the correct view. (We will get around to that eventually.) Rather, our initial goal is to force the Jehovah's Witness to prove that his view is correct. Shift the burden to his shoulders. He who makes a claim must defend it.

One good way to move the Jehovah's Witness to prove his point is to ask Columbo-like questions, such as "How did you come to that conclusion?" "Why do you believe that?" "What reasons can you give me that your view is correct?" "How do you know that is true?" These kinds of questions shift the burden of proof. In your zeal, your first inclination might be to launch immediately into a defense of the Christian faith. But be patient. You can do that soon enough. For now, invite the Jehovah's Witness to prove his point.

If he squirms and tries to wiggle out of answering your question, gently but persistently re-ask it. Do not allow him to make unsubstantiated claims without backing them up with hard proof. You might say something like this: "You've made a pretty strong claim that goes against traditional historic Christianity. I'm really interested in hearing the facts that back up your interpretation. I'm all ears."

Questions That Move the Conversation

The third type of Columbo-like question moves the conversation in a specific direction. This is called a *leading question*. These questions "often work better than statements to explain our view, to set up the discussion in a way that makes it easier for us to make our point, to soften our challenge to another's view, or to indirectly expose a flaw in the other's thinking."[8]

Before asking a leading question, you must first determine where you want the conversation to go. What point do you want to make? What conclusion do you want the Jehovah's Witness to draw? Once you make that determination, you can ask questions that move the conversation in that direction.

To illustrate, suppose I want to move the conversation in the direction of recognizing that Jesus is absolute deity and not just a lesser deity, as Jehovah's Witnesses believe. I might ask questions such as these: "Can you clear something up for me? Isaiah 44:24 says that God alone—and no other—is the Creator of all things. So how are we to take John 1:3 and Colossians 1:16, which tell us that Christ Himself created all things? Does this tell us something about Christ's identity as God?"

By asking such questions, I move the conversation to a topic that really matters. And the questions will cause the Jehovah's Witness to give serious thought about whether he or she has been taught the truth by the Watchtower Society.

My Goal in This Book

Watchtower literature affirms that Jehovah's Witnesses ought to be open to examining their faith to ensure that they are "in the truth."

> If we want to worship God acceptably, we must know the truth. This is an important issue. Our eternal happiness depends on it. Therefore, everyone should ask himself: "Is my way of worship acceptable to God? Am I genuinely interested in learning the truth of God's Word? Or am I afraid of what a careful investigation might reveal?"[9]

Jehovah's Witnesses are not only to carefully investigate and examine their faith with probing questions, they are also to make every effort to answer questions that other people ask them.

> When genuinely interested individuals ask for proof for the beliefs we hold dear, when they inquire about the false charges raised by opposers, it is our responsibility to defend our faith providing sound biblical answers. We are willing to give a clear explanation of our heartfelt convictions to others; indeed, we welcome the opportunity. Jehovah's organization does not discourage sincere, timely questions, as some opposers mistakenly claim.[10]

So by all means, ask questions. In part 2 of this book, I will provide plenty of examples of questions that are effective in evangelistic encounters with Jehovah's Witnesses.

When you ask such questions, the Jehovah's Witness may not necessarily go along with your point. But your question nevertheless could raise serious doubts in his or her mind. This is a good thing. The accumulative weight of many such questions is a powerful motivation for him or her to examine the truth claims of the Watchtower Society.

Note also that when you ask the Jehovah's Witness about any doctrine—salvation, the Holy Spirit, or the alleged inferiority of Jesus, for example—you will also want to include questions that reveal that the Watchtower Society is not a trustworthy source of truth. I say this because it is not enough for the Jehovah's Witness to see that he has some wrong doctrines. He must come to see that he cannot trust the Watchtower Society. So my general policy in every conversation I have with a Jehovah's Witness is (1) to challenge the credibility of the Watchtower Society and (2) to present the truth about at least one major doctrine. I will demonstrate how to do this in part 2 of the book.

4

The Importance of Effective Redirection

———∞∞∞———

Jehovah's Witnesses can begin a conversation on the doorstep in several different ways. Sometimes they start by making a point that puts the Watchtower Society in a favorable light. If they begin this way, I'm always willing to engage them. We saw in chapter 3 that my general policy in every conversation with Jehovah's Witnesses is to (1) challenge the trustworthiness of the Watchtower Society and to (2) correct their wrong view of at least one major doctrine. So if they begin their conversation with the Watchtower Society, I advise you to seize the moment. (I'll show you how to do this later in the book.)

On some occasions Jehovah's Witnesses begin the conversation on a matter of little importance. They might ring your doorbell and immediately talk about how evil blood transfusions are. Others start a conversation on why the US government is satanic. Others want to talk about why Christmas and Easter are pagan holidays and why God's true people should never celebrate them. Still others want to talk about the evils of birthdays. Certainly all these can be interesting discussions. But after a few minutes, redirect the conversation to more important topics of greater importance, such as…

- Who is the true God?
- Who is Jesus Christ?
- What did Jesus really accomplish in His death?
- What is the gospel of salvation?

Develop the skill of redirecting a conversation from matters of little significance to matters of great importance without seeming rude in the process. This is important. The time you have to talk with a Jehovah's Witness may be limited, so spend the majority of it on issues that really matter—that is, issues related to God, Jesus, and salvation.

How to Transition

When Jehovah's Witnesses ring the doorbell and you engage them in discussion, it is important not to be rude by changing the topic abruptly. If they start talking about a particular issue—let's say, blood transfusions—feel free to go along with them for a few minutes and discuss the issue.[1] But once you have chatted about the issue for a short time and you feel comfortable moving on, smoothly transition to a more important topic. The best way to do this is to use the topic they have brought up as a launchpad into your other topic. To illustrate, here is how I might use the issue of blood transfusions as a launchpad for a more important discussion.

> Well, all that is very interesting. Now that I think about it, all this talk about blood has brought to my mind the importance of the blood that Jesus Himself shed on our behalf to purchase our salvation. I am interested in your view about salvation in Jesus Christ. Can we chat about that for a few minutes?

Note that I related their topic to my topic. The connecting concept between the two discussions is blood. They wanted to talk about blood transfusions. I wanted to talk about the blood of Jesus and how it relates to the issue of salvation. So I made a smooth transition from their topic to my topic using the connecting concept of blood. And I did so without being offensive.

Let's consider a few more examples.

The Cross

Jehovah's Witnesses might begin conversations by alleging that the cross is a pagan symbol and that wearing a cross is a form of idolatry. In their view, Jesus was crucified on an upright stake. In this conversation, I would seek to accomplish two things:

- Address their faulty view of the cross.

- Transition from a discussion of the cross to a discussion of the salvation Jesus accomplished *at* the cross.

Here is how I might do it.

That's an interesting idea you have about Jesus dying on an upright stake. I know that Jehovah's Witnesses believe the Greek word for "cross" can mean "upright stake." But I've actually done a bit of research on this issue and have discovered that even though the word can refer to an upright stake, it is more commonly used for wooden structures that can look like a plus sign, a capital T, or a capital X. Were you aware of this? [Allow them to respond. After they respond, continue making your point.]

Here's something else I have discovered. If Jesus were crucified on an upright stake, only a single nail would be necessary to nail his hands to it. But John 20:25 says that "nails" were used. Doesn't that sound more like a crucifixion on a wooden structure shaped like a plus sign or maybe a capital T, with one nail being used for each hand? [Allow them to respond.]

Have you also considered that the Romans put a sign above Jesus's head, not above his hands, that said, "This is Jesus, the King of the Jews"? We see that in Matthew 27:37. How can that be reconciled with the idea that Jesus died on an upright stake, with his hands nailed above his head? [Again, allow them to respond. After they respond, make your transition.]

Well, our different opinions on this certainly make for an interesting debate. I guess the issue dearest to my own heart on all this is what Jesus actually accomplished in His death by crucifixion. Can I ask your opinion on Revelation 1:5? Speaking of Jesus, the text says, "To him who loves us and has freed us from our sins by his blood."

> A great cross-reference is Romans 5:9, which says, "We have now been justified by his blood." What's your take on these verses?

Notice that I related their topic to my topic. The connecting concept between the two discussions is the cross. They wanted to talk about the cross as a pagan symbol. I wanted to talk about the death Christ died on the cross and how it relates to the issue of salvation. So I used the concept of the cross to make a smooth transition from their topic to my topic.

In this case, my first goal was to plant a few seeds of doubt in their minds about their view of the cross itself. I certainly could have said much more on this issue (see my book *Reasoning from the Scriptures with the Jehovah's Witnesses*). But for the purpose of my conversation, it is enough to plant a few seeds of doubt and then transition to my main topic—the salvation Christ accomplished through His crucifixion. Without bringing any offense, I transitioned to a discussion on how our justification—that is, our acquittal of sin and our imputed righteousness—is based entirely on the blood Christ shed on our behalf. Now *that* is a conversation worth having!

Celebrating Christmas

Jehovah's Witnesses might also claim that Christmas is a pagan holiday and that God's people should not celebrate it. In this conversation, I would seek to accomplish two things:

- Address their faulty view of Christmas.
- Transition from a discussion of Christmas to a discussion of the importance of the birth of the Savior.

Here is how I would do it.

> That's an interesting claim. I know that Scripture never commands us to celebrate Christ's birth. But do you know

of a single Scripture that expressly prohibits God's people from celebrating Christ's birth?

[There is no such verse. If they give a verse against paganism, say, "That's a great verse on paganism. But again, do you know of a single Scripture that expressly prohibits God's people from celebrating Christ's birth?" They will probably stumble a bit. But at some point, they will probably say that December 25 is not the actual date of Christ's birth and that it is the same date of a Roman pagan holiday. If so, continue...]

Well, you may be right that Christ was not actually born on December 25. I know scholars have debated that issue, and most say we simply don't know the exact date of His birth. But I don't think that in itself means we should not celebrate Christmas on that date. The fact is, the early Christians refused to participate in the pagan ritual celebrated by the Romans on December 25. Their attitude was that if the pagans were going to celebrate their false religion, Christians should celebrate the one true religion. And what better way to celebrate than to focus attention on the birth of the Savior?

Regardless of any differences we may have on this issue, don't you think the more important issue is the actual birth of the Savior, Jesus Christ? Can I get your take on Acts 16:31? It says, "Believe in the Lord Jesus, and you will be saved." Do you think I can be saved by believing in Jesus the Savior?

Notice how I related their topic to my topic. The connecting concept between the two discussions is Christmas. They wanted to talk about Christmas as a pagan holiday. I wanted to talk about Christmas as the birth of the Savior, so I introduced a smooth transition from their topic to my topic.

In this case, my first goal was to plant a few seeds of doubt in their minds about their view of Christmas as a holiday. I then transitioned to my main topic—the birth of the Savior and how we are saved by trusting in Christ. Again, *that* is a conversation worth having!

I could give other illustrations, but I think you get the point. When they start a discussion about an issue of secondary importance, go ahead and converse about it for a short time. In the early part of the conversation, give your opinion on the immediate issue, but also be thinking about how you might transition to a topic of greater importance. That topic might be the gospel that saves, or the true Jesus, or the true God.

Reverse Redirection

I would be remiss not to mention that Jehovah's Witnesses themselves may seek to redirect the conversation if they feel cornered by one of your points. If you ask them a question they cannot answer, they may try to change the subject. If they do this, you can respectfully say something like this: "That's an interesting new issue, and I would really like to talk about it. Before we do that, though, let's finish up our previous discussion. I'm really interested in your views on it." Do not let them dodge the issues. Do not move on to a new topic of conversation until you are satisfied that you have effectively communicated the truth on the previous topic.

What If…?

What if the Jehovah's Witnesses who ring your doorbell actually start out on a topic of great importance, such as the doctrine of Jesus Christ or the gospel that saves? In that case, you will want to meet them on common ground but then move them to new ground. Let me explain.

The term "common ground" refers to fundamental beliefs that you agree on in at least a few areas. To find common ground means to find places where our beliefs intersect with those of Jehovah's Witnesses. As Norman and David Geisler put it, "Finding common ground involves discovering those mutually shared ideas that can be a springboard for deeper spiritual dialogue."[2]

For example, Jehovah's Witnesses believe in God, they believe in

Jesus, and they believe in salvation. Their views on these issues are heretical, but nevertheless they do believe these topics are important. These subjects can be starting points for our discussions.[3] Our goal is to meet them on common ground (focusing on their view of God, or Jesus, or the gospel that saves) and transition from there to new ground—the correct view on these issues.

The apostle Paul was a master at meeting people on common ground and then using that as a launchpad to share the truth. For example, he was "provoked within" when he entered Athens and observed that the city was full of idols (Acts 17:16). If he had acted upon his strong emotions, he probably would have vented his anger by blowing up at the Athenians. But he didn't. Instead, Paul sought a common ground from which he could communicate the good news of the gospel with these pagans.

Paul began his message, "Men of Athens, I perceive that in every way you are very religious. For as I passed along and observed the objects of your worship, I found also an altar with this inscription, 'To the unknown god.' What therefore you worship as unknown, this I proclaim to you" (verses 22-23).

Applying what we learn from Paul's encounter with the Athenians to present-day encounters with Jehovah's Witnesses, the wrong approach would be to vent our anger or be hostile. The right approach is to speak kindly and respectfully (as Paul did to the Athenians) and to use common ground as a launchpad to speak the truth.

Part 2 of this book will help you speak the truth effectively about a variety of critically important issues. In the next chapter, we will focus briefly on the importance of avoiding offense.

5

The Importance of Avoiding Offense

~∞∞~

Bringing offense is one of the most potent ways you can squash your evangelistic efforts. We can be 100 percent accurate in the doctrine that we share with someone, and we can be spot-on in our description of the gospel of salvation, but if we bring offense in the process of witnessing, our listeners will likely turn away and not come back. If we truly want to be effective as missionaries on our doorsteps, we must learn to avoid being offensive when we speak.

When I was new in the faith, I studied the Bible constantly. Whenever a cultist showed up on the doorstep, I never lost a theological argument. I look back on those early conversations with some regret because I now see that I fried people with correct doctrine. I now refer to this as the flamethrower method of evangelism. I never lost an argument, but I never witnessed a conversion to Christ. I was offensive in my approach. Please learn from my mistakes and do your best to avoid offense as you witness!

I have heard other Christians refer to the hammer approach to evangelism. When cultists show up on the doorstep, the Christian pounds them and pounds them with correct doctrine. Like the flamethrower method, the hammer method does not lead to conversion. It is depersonalizing and offensive, and cultists quickly quit listening to us. We must learn to see cultists not as the opposition but rather as lost people whom God loves and who desperately need to hear the truth.

Christian apologist Charles Strohmer tells an effective story to illustrate the problem.

> Remember those old World War II movies about submarines and warships? A submarine typically might be

floating on the surface of the ocean when suddenly enemy battleships appear on the horizon. A sudden sense of urgency strikes the men in the sub. They scurry to their posts, Klaxon horns blare ominously, and over the intercom the voice of the commander orders, "Dive! Dive!" The battleships meanwhile are steaming furiously toward the sub, intending to blast a few holes into its side.

Too often Christians look like those warships to non-Christian spiritual seekers, who cannot move fast enough to get out of our line of fire! We begin a conversation, the person starts listening, but then we do or say something, usually unwittingly, that sends the wrong signal to the person's radar. It's a common dynamic. We are perceived as dangerous, and the person dives below the surface of communication, effectively insulated from really hearing what we are saying. The person is no longer actively listening. If we continue to be menacing, he or she will mentally move leagues away, even though physically present.[1]

We need to handle our conversations in a way that invites Jehovah's Witnesses to keep floating on the surface of communication. We ought to make every effort to avoid flooding their radar with threatening comments. Let's convey the appearance not of a battleship but of a rescue ship en route to the heavenly country. If we handle ourselves rightly, they may accept our invitation to come aboard our rescue ship.

What happens if you slip up and suddenly recognize that you have inadvertently brought offense? In a word, apologize! Say something like, "You know, I have the feeling I just upset you. I didn't mean to. I'm sorry about that." Or you might say, "I have the feeling we may be misunderstanding each other. Do you feel that way too? Why don't we backtrack and start over on this part of the conversation? Are you game?" If you don't apologize, you may erect an emotional barrier that will thwart the rest of your conversation. So be humble and do the right thing. Apologize if you have brought offense.

The Bible says a great deal about avoiding offense with the tongue. Here's a brief summary of the more important verses.

Reckless Words Can Pierce the Soul

"There is one whose rash words are like sword thrusts, but the tongue of the wise brings healing" (Proverbs 12:18). Thoughtless words can wound people's emotions. By contrast, thoughtful words—typically spoken by wise people—bring healing to one's emotions. "Some people's normal speech pattern is constantly to accuse, belittle, manipulate, mock, insult, or condemn, and their rash words hurt other people and feel like sword thrusts. This is opposite of the way of wisdom taught in Proverbs, for the tongue of the wise brings healing."[2]

The Mouth Must Be Guarded

"Set a guard, O Lord, over my mouth; keep watch over the door of my lips!" (Psalm 141:3). The psalmist wanted God to providentially keep him from speaking inappropriate or incautious words. He knew of the human tendency to inadvertently wound others with the tongue. You and I may not necessarily intend to speak inappropriate words to a Jehovah's Witness on the doorstep, but it is certainly possible that we could do so inadvertently, thereby bringing a sudden end to our conversation. Let's follow the lead of the psalmist by asking God to set a guard over our mouths.

Keep a Tight Rein on Your Tongue

"If anyone thinks he is religious and does not bridle his tongue but deceives his heart, this person's religion is worthless" (James 1:26). Just as a rider uses a bridle to control a horse, so you and I must make concerted efforts to control our tongues. And just as a horse without restraint could gallop off in any direction, so a tongue without restraint could go off in any direction and bring offense to others. We bridle our tongues by using them according to the instructive constraints Scripture provides.

A Gentle Answer Turns Away Wrath

"A soft answer turns away wrath, but a harsh word stirs up anger" (Proverbs 15:1). A soft answer is a gentle answer. One Bible scholar notes that "a gentle answer can dispel a potentially tense situation by dissolving a person's wrath. Being conciliatory in such a situation requires forethought, patience, self-control, and kindness, virtues commonly lauded in Proverbs."[3] Gideon's soft answer yielded peace (Judges 8:1-3).

The phrase "harsh word" literally means "word of pain," or "word that is hurtful." Understandably, hurtful words quickly yield anger. Nabal's harsh words put David in a fighting mood (1 Samuel 25:10-13).

Let's resolve to use soft and gentle words in all our witnessing encounters.

Soft Speech Crushes Strong Opposition

"A soft tongue will break a bone" (Proverbs 25:15). This sounds strange at first reading. But in context, it makes perfect sense. Obviously, words can never actually break a bone. But the idea is that words can accomplish what is often considered insurmountable. As *The Bible Knowledge Commentary* puts it, "Patience and a gentle tongue can be unusually influential, accomplishing far more than loss of temper and harsh words…The idea is that softly spoken words can accomplish difficult things."[4]

This verse has particular relevance to conversing with Jehovah's Witnesses. Bible expositor D.A. Garrett explains that "the bones are the most rigid body parts inside of a person, and fracturing the bones here refers to breaking down the deepest, most hardened resistance to an idea a person may possess."[5] By communicating the truth of Scripture using gentle words, we can slowly erode and break down the resistance in the Jehovah's Witness's heart.

The Tongue Can Destroy

"The tongue is a small part of the body, but it makes great boasts. Consider what a great forest is set on fire by a small spark. The tongue also is a fire, a world of evil among the parts of the body. It corrupts the whole body, sets the whole course of one's life on fire, and is itself set on fire by hell" (James 3:5-6 NIV). This passage reveals that "though small and comparatively insignificant, the tongue can effect great change out of all proportion to its size...The tongue has as much destructive power as a spark in a forest. It is petite but powerful."[6]

Someone said that "the tongue is but three inches long, yet it can kill a man six feet high." Never forget that the tongue can cut like a sharp razor (Psalm 52:2), can sting like a poisonous snake (Psalm 140:3), and can kill (Proverbs 18:21). No one can tame it (James 3:8).

The relevance for witnessing to Jehovah's Witnesses is simply this: Choose your words carefully and deliberately. My best advice is to be humble, patient, and kind in all that you do and say.

The Power of Words

Earlier in the chapter I noted Charles Strohmer's excellent analogy of Christians and cultists as battleships and submarines. He goes on to tell a story of how he once debated a professional psychic on live radio in Nottingham, England. This psychic had a strong animosity toward Christians and Christianity. Strohmer picked up on this as the debate unfolded. About halfway through the debate, he gently asked her whether she had ever been hurt by a Christian. She was silent for a few seconds. The question penetrated deep into her emotions. She then conceded being hurt by a number of Christians. Strohmer discussed these incidents with her for a few minutes and then said to her, "I want to apologize to you for those Christians who've treated you poorly. Please forgive us." The lady responded affirmatively, and her whole demeanor altered.

Afterward, once outside of the soundproof studio, the woman confided, "Because I've been so hurt by Christians, I almost didn't accept the offer to debate you. But now I'd like to ask if we could keep talking. Are you busy this afternoon?"[7]

Strohmer did it right. Let's follow his lead!

6

The Importance of Speech Peppered by Grace

⎯⎯ ∞ ⎯⎯

One of the most important apologetics passages in the New Testament is Colossians 4:5-6, where the apostle Paul instructs us, "Conduct yourselves with wisdom toward outsiders, making the most of the opportunity. Let your speech always be with grace, as though seasoned with salt, so that you will know how you should respond to each person." I am convinced that apologists would be far more effective in their efforts today if they'd make this passage the heart of their modus operandi. So important is this passage that I want to devote this entire chapter to briefly mining its riches.

Wisdom Toward Outsiders

Our passage begins with the exhortation, "Conduct yourselves with wisdom toward outsiders." The apostle Paul—himself a Hebrew of Hebrews (Philippians 3:5) and an Old Testament scholar par excellence—spoke about wisdom against a Jewish backdrop. The main Hebrew word for wisdom in the Old Testament is *hokmah*. It was used commonly for the skill of craftsmen, sailors, singers, administrators, and counselors. *Hokmah* pointed to the experience and efficiency of these various workers in using their skills. Similarly, a person who possesses *hokmah* in his spiritual life and relationship to God is both knowledgeable and experienced in following God's way. Biblical wisdom involves skill in the art of godly living. This wisdom is broad in its scope, teaching students how to be successful at home, at work, in human relationships, and in regard to money, death and the afterlife, and much more (see Proverbs 1–9).

It is against this backdrop that Colossians 4:5-6 takes on significance. We are to use God-informed and God-influenced skill in our interactions with others. It is my hope and prayer that this book will help you attain that wisdom in dealing with Jehovah's Witnesses.

Make the Most of Every Opportunity

Being wise includes "making the most of the opportunity." This is the underlying reason for my view that every time a Jehovah's Witness shows up on your doorstep, you are being given a kingdom assignment. The truth is, you do not know if you will ever see that person again. It thus makes good sense to make the most of the opportunity by sharing the truth of Scripture with him or her.

This verse is also one of the underlying reasons for my advice in a previous chapter to redirect conversations to issues that really matter. If the Jehovah's Witness wants to talk about blood transfusions, use that as a launchpad into a topic that really matters—such as the blood of Christ and its role in our salvation. We do not make the most of our opportunities by spending a lot of time discussing issues of little importance.

As I write, I am aware that one day you and I will face Christ at the judgment seat of Christ (Romans 14:10; 1 Corinthians 3:10-15; 2 Corinthians 5:10). At that judgment we will receive or lose rewards based on how we lived as Christians. We will surely answer for the way we responded to every witnessing opportunity.

One of the ways we make the most out of all our witnessing opportunities is to prepare in advance for them. That is one of the reasons I wrote this book—to help you prepare in advance for witnessing to Jehovah's Witnesses.

Gracious Speech

Our passage goes on to tell us, "Let your speech always be with grace." The word "speech" in this verse literally means "word, discourse, talking." It refers to any conversation the Christian has but especially to those in witnessing or evangelistic contexts. We are to be gracious toward others because God Himself is gracious to us. We ought to reflect the graciousness of God in all our encounters with people. The word "grace" in the context of Colossians 4:6 carries the idea of "pleasing, pleasant, charming, and winsome."[1] Our conversations with Jehovah's Witnesses ought to be brimming with such characteristics.

Speech Seasoned with Salt

The apostle Paul then tells us that our speech or conversation ought to be "seasoned with salt." Bible scholars note that the metaphor of salt might carry a number of meanings. Some suggest that since salt makes food more attractive and appealing (Matthew 5:13), the metaphor in Colossians 4:5-6 may indicate that our speech is to be attractive and wholesome (Ephesians 4:29).[2] Others suggest that speech that is "seasoned with salt" may metaphorically refer to "speaking in an interesting, stimulating, and wise way."[3] Still others suggest that since salt retards spoilage, the metaphor might indicate that "our speech should be tempered so as never to be insipid, corrupt, or obscene."[4] Perhaps all of these nuances of meaning have relevance in the present context.

Prepared with an Answer

Our passage closes by informing us that all of this is "so that you will know how you should respond to each person." This is clearly an apologetics context—providing answers for the faith. This verse reminds me of 1 Peter 3:15-16, which instructs us, "Always [be] prepared to make a defense to anyone who asks you for a reason for the hope that is in you; yet do it with gentleness and respect." Such verses make it clear that it is not just what we say that is important, but also how we say it. Christian apologist Adam Pelser put it this way:

> Paul thus emphasizes that the manner of one's presentation and defense of the gospel is often as crucial as its content and that the character of the evangelist-apologist is of first importance. It is not enough to be equipped with apologetic reasons in defense of the faith; we must also live attractive apologetic lives. Not only must we become equipped to know what to say to unbelievers, we must also learn how to say it. In order to make the most of every

> evangelistic opportunity we must season our conversations
> with the pleasing flavor of salt.[5]

Pelser then utilizes the word "salt" as an acronym to help us remember things that ought to characterize our speech in witnessing encounters.

Sensitivity. We ought to be sensitive in our personal evangelism and witnessing. This means that we not only speak but also listen. As well, we ought to engage in evangelism with gentle hands, so to speak. We must be sensitive to the opinions, feelings, and hurts of others. A good apologist is a sensitive apologist.

Applicability. We must seek to present apologetic answers that are applicable and relevant to our hearers. In the context of Jehovah's Witnesses, our goal is not only to defend the truth of biblical Christianity but also to specifically answer the objections they have to some of the doctrines of orthodox Protestant Christianity, such as the Trinity, the absolute deity of Jesus Christ, and salvation through grace alone by faith alone.

Love. It has often been said that cultists do not care how much you know until they know how much you care (see Matthew 22:39). Though it is an overused phrase, it is as true and relevant as ever. A good apologist is a loving apologist (see 1 Corinthians 13:1). Love helps to bring down barriers to communication, whereas in-your-face apologetics erects those barriers. By using love in our apologetics, we are reflecting God's own character. Jesus Himself was love incarnate. We are ambassadors for Christ (2 Corinthians 5:20), so we ought to represent His love to others.

Truth. While we are to be loving, we are also to tell the truth. In fact, our love compels us to tell others the truth. Only an unloving person would withhold the truth that leads to eternal life. When we communicate the truth, however, we are to speak the truth in love (Ephesians 4:15).

Job once asked, "Can that which is tasteless be eaten without salt...? My appetite refuses to touch them; they are as food that is loathsome to me" (Job 6:6-7). Just as food without salt can seem unpalatable, so conversation that lacks love, sensitivity, and pleasantness can be unpalatable to our hearers. Never forget that a good apologist is not just one who has all the right answers. He is also a person who communicates those answers in a God-honoring way.

Saving Face

Only after a number of very patient witnessing encounters will some Jehovah's Witnesses concede defeat and open themselves to the true Jesus and the true gospel. As Wilbur Lingle put it so well, "It takes from six months to a year, or even longer, before a person becomes a Jehovah's Witness. It is, therefore, unrealistic to expect he will come out after only a few attempts at witnessing to him. It will take a lot of time, love, patience, study and prayer."[6] This calls for lots of grace on your part.

Showing grace in our conversations and being sensitive includes helping the Jehovah's Witness to save face. I picked up this tidbit of advice from my old friend Walter Martin. He said that when you share the gospel with a Jehovah's Witness and defend your position from Scripture, you will eventually know that you have won the argument. When that moment arrives, you must make every effort to let love shine through and allow the other person to save face. Otherwise, the Jehovah's Witness will resent you and fight you even though he knows in his heart that you are right. Walter suggested handling it this way:

> When you sense that the person has lost the argument and is deflated, that's the time to be magnanimous and say to the person, lovingly: "I realize that we can get awfully uptight in these areas if we let ourselves. Let's just forget that you are a Jehovah's Witness and I am a Baptist (or whatever you are). And let's just think of ourselves as two people who want more than anything else to know the whole truth and the whole counsel of God. Right?" I haven't met a cultist yet who wouldn't say "Right" in response.[7]

Disarming the situation in this way will help lower defensive barriers and will create an atmosphere in which the Jehovah's Witness will actually want to hear what you have to say.

Former Jehovah's Witness David Reed attests to the importance of taking a loving, disarming approach. He points out that "empathy is so very important when reaching out to these misled individuals. Try to think of how you would want others to speak to you, if you were the one who was misled. Then remember that 'all things whatsoever ye would that men should do to you, do ye even so to them' (Matt. 7:12)."[8]

The psalmist once said to God, "Let the words of my mouth and the meditation of my heart be acceptable in your sight" (Psalm 19:14). This ought to be our prayer every time we converse with Jehovah's Witnesses. Reflecting the spirit of this verse, Frederick Faber—a British hymn writer who lived in the 1800s—said, "Kindness has converted more sinners than zeal, eloquence, or learning." To be sure, our biblical answers are critically important. But so is kindness. Never forget this equation:

Strong biblical answers + gentleness, respect, and kindness = Christian apologist.

7

The Importance of Your Testimony

⎯⎯⎯⎯∞⎯⎯⎯⎯

Giving your personal testimony is an important component of any witnessing encounter. In my own case, throughout my childhood and teenage years I thought I was a Christian because I regularly attended church. For years I participated in various church activities, sang in the church choir, and went through all the motions. I even went through a confirmation ceremony at my church—an event that was supposed to confirm that in fact I was a Christian. I had no idea at that time that I really was not a Christian according to the biblical definition of the term.

Like so many others today, I was under the illusion that a Christian was someone who attended church or subscribed to a Christian code of ethics and performed good works. I believed that as long as I somewhat consistently lived my life according to this code of ethics, I was surely a Christian. I believed that as long as my good deeds outweighed my bad deeds by the time I died, I could look forward to a destiny in heaven.

It was not until years later that I came to understand that the mere act of going to church does not make me a Christian. As the great evangelist Billy Sunday (1862–1935) put it, "Going to church doesn't make you a Christian any more than going to a garage makes you an automobile."

I came to see that most fundamentally a Christian is one who has a personal, ongoing relationship with Jesus. This relationship begins the moment one places faith in Christ for salvation. It has been well said that Christianity is not so much a religion as it is a relationship.

The Word "Christian"

It is fascinating to me that the word "Christian" is used only three times in the New Testament—the most important of which is Acts

11:26 (see also Acts 26:28 and 1 Peter 4:16). And it is instructive to observe just what this word meant among those to whom the term was originally applied. By so doing, we can see whether we ourselves are Christians according to the biblical definition.

In Acts 11:26, we are told simply and straightforwardly, "In Antioch the disciples were first called Christians." This would have been around AD 42, about a decade after Christ died on the cross and was resurrected from the dead.

Until this time the followers of Jesus had referred to themselves as brothers (Acts 15:1,23), disciples (Acts 9:26), believers (Acts 5:14), and saints (Romans 8:27). But now, in Antioch, they are also called Christians.

What does the term mean? The answer is found in the "ian" ending. Among the ancients this ending meant "belonging to the party of." "Herodians" belonged to the party of Herod. "Caesarians" belonged to the party of Caesar. "Christians" belonged to Christ. And Christians were loyal to Christ, just as the Herodians were loyal to Herod and Caesarians were loyal to Caesar.

The significance of the word "Christian" is that these followers of Jesus were recognized as a distinct group. They were seen as distinct from Judaism and as distinct from all other religions of the ancient world. We might loosely translate the term Christian, "those belonging to Christ," "Christ ones," or perhaps "Christ people." They are ones who follow Christ.

Try to imagine a resident of Antioch asking his neighbor, "Who are these people?" "Oh, these are the people who are always talking about Christ—the Christ-people, the Christians."

Those who have studied the culture of Antioch have noted that the Antiochans were well known for making fun of people. It may be that local residents applied the word "Christian" to the early followers of Jesus as a term of derision, an appellation of ridicule. Be that as it may, history reveals that by the second century, Christians adopted the title as a badge of honor. They took pride (in a healthy way) in following Jesus. They had a genuine relationship with the living, resurrected Christ, and they were utterly faithful to Him, even in the face of death.

When I finally came to understand this, it struck me just how shallow my confirmation ceremony as a youngster had been. I came to see that Christianity is not about me and my ethics. Rather, it's all about Jesus and my personal relationship with Him.

Jehovah's Witnesses Desperately Need to Hear

I mention all this because your personal testimony to a Jehovah's Witness must include the fact that you are sure of going to heaven precisely because you have a personal relationship with Jesus Christ, the divine Savior and Redeemer, who died for you at the cross. Great Christians throughout church history have long emphasized that Christianity most fundamentally involves such a personal relationship.

- "Christianity is neither a creed nor a ceremonial, but life vitally connected with a loving Christ" (Josiah Strong, 1847–1916).

- "Christianity is not the acceptance of certain ideas. It is a personal attitude of trust and devotion to a person" (Stephen Neill).

- "A Christian is, in essence, somebody personally related to Jesus Christ," and "Christianity without Christ is a chest without a treasure, a frame without a portrait, a corpse without breath" (John R.W. Stott).

- "Christianity is not devotion to work, or to a cause, or a doctrine, but devotion to a person, the Lord Jesus Christ" (Oswald Chambers, 1874–1917).

- "Christianity isn't only going to church on Sunday. It is living twenty-four hours of every day with Jesus Christ" (Billy Graham).

So as you give your testimony, make a conscious effort to center it on Jesus Christ, His gracious gift of salvation based on His death at the cross, and your personal relationship with Him.

The Biblical Case for Giving Testimony

There is a strong biblical precedent for God's people telling others about what God has done in their lives. We are to follow their example. Consider these representative verses.

- "Oh give thanks to the LORD; call upon his name; make known his deeds among the peoples!…Tell of all his wondrous works" (1 Chronicles 16:8-9).

- "Tell among the peoples his deeds" (Psalm 9:11).

- "Come, let us declare in Zion the work of the LORD our God" (Jeremiah 51:10).

- "Everyone who acknowledges me before men, I also will acknowledge before my Father who is in heaven" (Matthew 10:32).

- "'Go home to your friends and tell them how much the Lord has done for you, and how he has had mercy on you.' And he went away and began to proclaim in the Decapolis how much Jesus had done for him, and everyone marveled" (Mark 5:19-20).

- "You are witnesses of these things" (Luke 24:48).

- "The woman left her water jar and went away into town and said to the people, 'Come, see a man who told me all that I ever did. Can this be the Christ?' They went out of the town and were coming to him…Many Samaritans from that town believed in him because of the woman's testimony, 'He told me all that I ever did'" (John 4:28-30,39).

- "Do not be ashamed of the testimony about our Lord" (2 Timothy 1:8).

- "Always [be] prepared to make a defense to anyone who asks you for a reason for the hope that is in you" (1 Peter 3:15).

Such verses remind me that Christ has called us to be a light to the world around us. "You are the light of the world. A city set on a hill cannot be hidden" (Matthew 5:14). Jesus did not call us to be secret-agent Christians. We are not to cloak our lights. Someone once said, "No one is a light unto himself, not even the sun." The darkness of the cults is hovering over Western culture as never before, so the light of each Christian has never been needed more. As Billy Graham put it, "The Christian should stand out like a sparkling diamond."

You and I are called to be personal witnesses of Jesus Christ. Just before ascending into heaven, Jesus instructed His disciples, "You will receive power when the Holy Spirit has come upon you, and you will be my witnesses in Jerusalem and in all Judea and Samaria, and to the end of the earth" (Acts 1:8). A witness is a person who testifies. Christians testify about Jesus—who He is, what He has done, and their personal relationship with Him.

A Christian leader once said, "Every heart with Christ is a missionary; every heart without Christ is a mission field." Christians can be testifying missionaries wherever they are, whether abroad or at home. We can be missionaries to Jehovah's Witnesses when they show up on the doorstep. And when they do, we must be ready to share the good news and describe the impact it has made in our own lives.

When you tell others about what the Lord has done in your life, speak with conviction. Remember, you may not be an authority about what every single verse in the Bible means, but you are an authority on what Jesus has personally done in your life. More specifically, you are an authority on how you were once a lost sinner, and how Jesus rescued you from sin and gave you eternal salvation. In our day of relativism, when there is so much confusion about so many things, a testimony delivered with conviction will be noticed.

I can assure you that the average Jehovah's Witness will be intensely interested as you share your testimony. Wilbur Lingle, who has broad experience in witnessing to Jehovah's Witnesses, makes this comment:

> I usually take thirty minutes to give my testimony. I try to make it as interesting as possible. I want them to feel what

I went through when I realized the heaviness of the burden of my sin. I want them to understand the relief I felt when I recognized and confessed my sins, trusted Jesus Christ as my personal Savior, and had this burden removed. I want them to long for the love, joy, and peace with God I experienced. They usually listen intently as I'm giving my testimony, often sitting on the edge of the couch.[1]

What to Include in Your Testimony

When giving your testimony, be sure to share what your life was like before you were a Christian, how you became a Christian, and what your life has been like since becoming a Christian. More specifically…

- Describe what your life was like before you were a Christian. What were your feelings, attitudes, actions, and relationships like during this time? The apostle Paul clearly described what his life was like before he was a Christian (Acts 26:4-11.)

- What events in your life led up to your decision to trust in Christ? What caused you to begin considering Christ as a solution to your needs? Was there a crisis? A lack of meaning in life? A pervasive awareness of sin? A fear of death and what lies beyond? Be specific.

- Describe your conversion experience. Were you at home? Were you in a church? Were other Christians with you at the time? The apostle Paul, in his testimony, clearly spoke of how he became a Christian (Acts 26:12-18.)

- What kind of change took place in your life following your conversion? What effect did trusting in Christ have on your feelings, attitudes, actions, and relationships? Paul spoke of how his life changed once he became a Christian (Acts 26:19-23).

What to Avoid

You should try to avoid certain things when sharing your personal testimony.

- Do not be too long-winded. People have short attention spans. Unless they indicate they want every detail, try to cover the essential points within a half hour.

- Try not to use "Christianese." In other words, do not use too much theological language that your listener may be unfamiliar with—words like justification, propitiation, reconciliation, and sanctification. If you do use such words, be sure to clearly define what you mean by them.

- Do not imply that true Christianity is a bed of roses for believers. Such a claim is simply not true. You might even share some of the struggles you have endured since becoming a Christian. Your listener may identify with what you have experienced.

- Do not be ignorant of or insensitive to the Jehovah's Witness's legalistic spiritual blindness. "The natural person does not accept the things of the Spirit of God, for they are folly to him, and he is not able to understand them because they are spiritually discerned" (1 Corinthians 2:14). The gospel of God's grace may not make much sense to one who has been thoroughly schooled in a gospel of works. For this reason, devote a good part of your testimony to how the gospel of God's grace has set you free.

You might close your testimony by asking the Jehovah's Witness if he or she is interested in meeting the Jesus who set you free.

PART 2

Conversations on the Big Issues

In each of the following chapters, you'll be able to eavesdrop on conversations with Jehovah's Witnesses. As you read through each conversation, notice that...

1. My strategy in each conversation is to (1) show that the Watchtower Society is not a trustworthy source of truth and (2) share the truth about at least one major doctrine. Pay careful attention to how I do this. Burn this two-fold strategy into your mind.

2. Because Jehovah's Witnesses often begin conversations on matters of little importance, most of the following conversations begin with topics of lesser importance and transition to more important topics.

3. I ask questions that accomplish three things—find facts, shift the burden of proof, and change the direction of the conversation (see chapter 4). If you read carefully, you'll witness all three in action in each of the conversations.

8

Conversations About the Watchtower Society

⟨⟨⟩⟩

The Watchtower Society exercises authority over all Jehovah's Witnesses. It was founded by Charles Taze Russell (1852–1916), who was raised as a Presbyterian. As a teenager, Russell became increasingly bothered by the doctrines of predestination and eternal punishment, and he decided to leave the Presbyterian church. He tried the Congregational church for a while but became a religious skeptic at age 17. He studied many religions during this period but found none that satisfied him.

Eventually Russell came into contact with some Adventists who were excited about Bible prophecy, and this began his lifelong interest in prophecy. In 1879 he began publishing a magazine titled *Zion's Watch Tower and Herald of Christ's Presence*, which would eventually evolve into *The Watchtower* magazine. His influence began to grow. In various cities, congregations began cropping up that were committed to Russell's interpretation of prophecy.

In 1881, Russell founded Zion's Watch Tower Tract Society in Pittsburgh, Pennsylvania. He quickly enlisted hundreds of evangelists to go door to door, distributing the prophetic literature published by the society. He later set up offices in New York.

Over the next few decades, Russell did a great deal of writing. He completed his six-volume *Studies in the Scriptures* by 1904 and claimed that if his followers read these six books alone, without even opening the Bible, they would have the light of the Scriptures. If on the other hand they read the Bible alone without reading his books, they would be in darkness within two years.[1]

After Russell died, Joseph "Judge" Rutherford (1869–1942) assumed leadership of the Watchtower Society. A micromanager at heart, Rutherford transitioned the society into a tight-knit hierarchical organization. During this time, when Jehovah's Witnesses went door to door, they played phonograph recordings of Rutherford's sermons on the doorstep. An appeal was then made to purchase a Watchtower book.

Upon Rutherford's death, Nathan Knorr (1905–1977) became president. Knorr was a practical businessman and good administrator. He ended the use of phonographs on doorsteps and instead trained Jehovah's Witnesses to communicate the Watchtower message. Under his leadership, the Jehovah's Witness Bible—the New World Translation—was produced.

Frederick Franz (1893–1992) took the reins after Knorr died. He was probably the most theologically astute president the Watchtower Society ever had. Following his death, Milton Henschel—a third-generation Jehovah's Witness—became president. In 2000, Don Adams, a 50-year Watchtower veteran, became the president following Henschel's resignation.

Today the Watchtower Society governs all Jehovah's Witnesses worldwide. It claims to be God's visible representative on earth. The Society is "an organization to direct the minds of God's people."[2] "Jehovah's organization...should influence our every decision."[3] "Unless we are in touch with this channel of communication that God is using, we will not progress along the road to life, no matter how much Bible reading we do."[4]

Through the Watchtower Society and no other, God allegedly teaches the Bible to humankind today. "Only this organization functions for Jehovah's purpose and to his praise. To it alone God's Sacred Word, the Bible, is not a sealed book."[5] The Watchtower Society is "the one and only channel which the Lord has used in dispensing his truth continually since the beginning of the harvest period."[6]

Without the vast literature produced by the Watchtower Society, people would supposedly not be able to understand the Bible. Other Christian organizations are viewed as deceptive, rooted in the work of the devil. "Jehovah's organization alone, in all the earth, is directed by

God's holy spirit or active force."[7] "We must not lose sight of the fact that God is directing his organization."[8]

Jehovah's Witnesses are expected to obey the Watchtower Society in all matters, and they are to engage in Bible study that depends on the Watchtower Society. "God has not arranged for [His] Word to speak independently or to shine forth life-giving truths by itself. It is through his organization God provides this light."[9] "Avoid independent thinking...questioning the counsel that is provided by God's visible organization."[10]

Should one choose to disobey the voice of Jehovah as manifested in the Watchtower Society, one is disfellowshipped and shunned.

Falsehoods to Watch For

- The Watchtower Society is Jehovah's mouthpiece on earth, just like a prophet.
- All other Christian organizations are deceptive and are of the devil.
- God's people are to engage in Bible study that depends on the Watchtower Society.
- Reading the Bible alone (without Watchtower literature) will lead one astray.
- God's true followers—the Jehovah's Witnesses—must unquestioningly obey the Watchtower or are disfellowshipped and shunned.

Important Points to Introduce

Here are some essential points to emphasize and support during conversations with Jehovah's Witnesses.

- The Watchtower Society is a human institution. It does not speak for God.
- The Watchtower misinterprets a number of Bible verses in building support for its authority.

- People do not need the Watchtower Society in order to understand the Bible.

Eavesdropping on a Conversation

JEHOVAH'S WITNESS: Good morning. My name is Lou. Do you have a few minutes to chat?

CHRISTIAN: Sure. What's up? [Silently pray the open-the-heart prayer I mentioned in the introduction.]

JEHOVAH'S WITNESS: Has it ever bothered you how many so-called Christian ministers and pastors charge money for their services? They are profiting off of the kingdom of God. You'd think that if they were true representatives of Jehovah, they wouldn't charge people money for it. That's one reason I joined the Jehovah's Witnesses, who don't have a paid clergy. They only request small donations to cover the cost of the printed magazines and books that are distributed throughout neighborhoods.

CHRISTIAN: So, let me get this straight. You think it is wrong for a pastor of a local church to receive a salary?

JEHOVAH'S WITNESS: Yes. Isn't that what the Bible teaches?

CHRISTIAN: Well, that's a good question. I know the Jehovah's Witnesses have their own Bible called the New World Translation. Would you mind if I quote a verse to you from my Bible—the English Standard Version?

JEHOVAH'S WITNESS: That's fine.

CHRISTIAN: In 1 Corinthians 9:13-14 the apostle Paul said, "Do you not know that those who are employed in the temple service get their food from the temple, and those who serve at the altar share in the sacrificial offerings? In the same way, the Lord commanded that those who proclaim the gospel should get their living by the gospel." What's your take on those verses?

JEHOVAH'S WITNESS: Hmm…I'm not sure I've seen those verses before.

CHRISTIAN: These verses do not say pastors are profiting off of the kingdom of God. But they are to "get their living" by doing the work of ministry. Do you see anything wrong with that?

JEHOVAH'S WITNESS: Well, not when you put it that way.

CHRISTIAN: I don't either. So even though Jehovah's Witness clergy are unpaid, that in itself doesn't prove that they are the only true clergy, right?

JEHOVAH'S WITNESS: Well, there are other things to consider.

CHRISTIAN: Okay. I'd love to talk to you about those other things. But first, can I ask you another question about the Watchtower Society? Isn't it true that the members of the governing body are supported by the organization? And aren't the Jehovah's Witnesses' "circuit overseers" on the payroll as well? I'm wondering how this relates to your negative feelings about Christian pastors and ministers who are paid for what they do.

JEHOVAH'S WITNESS: Well, they're not paid very much.

CHRISTIAN: But they are paid, right?

JEHOVAH'S WITNESS: I guess they are. But they're in a special leadership position.

CHRISTIAN: [Smile.] Pastors are in a position of leadership too. By the way, did you know that Mormons don't have a paid clergy? Does that mean Mormons are the true people of God?

JEHOVAH'S WITNESS: Ha ha. Okay, I see your point. But surely you are not denying that there is financial abuse among people in Christian ministry.

CHRISTIAN: That's a fair point. There are definitely some bogus Christian preachers out there—especially some of the ones you see at night on TV. Some of these people are definitely in love with money. Those folks are as distasteful to me as they are to you. But don't let them sour your view of all Christian ministers and pastors, most of whom are faithful servants of God. In any event, a moment ago you said there were other things to consider. You've got me curious. What did you have in mind?

JEHOVAH'S WITNESS: Well, we believe that Scripture itself indicates that God's people need help from God's organization—the Watchtower Society—in order to properly understand Scripture.

CHRISTIAN: Where do you see that in the Bible?

JEHOVAH'S WITNESS: For one thing, Acts 8:30-31 reveals that an Ethiopian man needed help understanding Scripture.

CHRISTIAN: I grant you that. But on what basis do you conclude that this passage demands the need for an organization like the Watchtower Society?

JEHOVAH'S WITNESS: Well, the meaning of Scripture is not always self-evident to people, and so they need help to understand it.

CHRISTIAN: Okay. I see where you're coming from. But let's look carefully at the text. Who helped the Ethiopian man—an organization or a man named Philip?

JEHOVAH'S WITNESS: Well, in this case, Philip.

CHRISTIAN: Right. One man helped another man. One man taught another man. But there is nothing in these verses about the Watchtower Society.

JEHOVAH'S WITNESS: Well, the passage points to the need of being helped to understand Scripture. That's why the Watchtower Society exists.

CHRISTIAN: I agree that the passage points to the need of being helped to understand Scripture. That's why Scripture says in Ephesians 4:11 and elsewhere that God has given the gift of teaching to certain Christians who can then help others understand Scripture. That's what happened in Acts 8:30-31. Philip taught the Ethiopian man what he needed to know. The man then acted upon what he learned by confessing his faith in Jesus Christ for salvation and getting baptized. We see that in Acts 8:34-38. What happened next with the Ethiopian man, according to verse 39?

JEHOVAH'S WITNESS: It says he went on his way.

CHRISTIAN: Right. He went on his way. Is there any indication that he had to join or submit to an organization?

JEHOVAH'S WITNESS: No. But again, just as Philip helped the Ethiopian man understand Scripture, so the Watchtower Society helps people today to understand Scripture.

CHRISTIAN: [Smile.] I understand what you're saying. But you're also saying that people today cannot understand Scripture without the help of the Watchtower Society, right?

JEHOVAH'S WITNESS: That's what we believe.

CHRISTIAN: But there's no explicit support for the Watchtower in this verse, right?

JEHOVAH'S WITNESS: I understand your point.

CHRISTIAN: There's a verse I want to share with you. It's 2 Timothy 3:15-17, where the apostle Paul said to Timothy, "You have been acquainted with the sacred writings, which are able to make you wise for salvation through faith in Christ Jesus. All Scripture is breathed out by God and profitable for teaching, for reproof, for correction, and for training in righteousness, that the man of God may be competent, equipped for every good work." Here is my question: Were the Scriptures alone sufficient for young Timothy to understand salvation in Christ?

JEHOVAH'S WITNESS: Okay, I see your point. But again, people generally need help in understanding Scripture, and that's why they need the Watchtower Society.

CHRISTIAN: In Timothy's case, Scripture alone was sufficient to help him understand salvation in Jesus Christ. That being so, isn't Scripture alone sufficient to help you and me understand salvation in Jesus Christ?

JEHOVAH'S WITNESS: I understand your point.

CHRISTIAN: [Smile.] The Berean Christians also used Scripture alone. In fact, according to Acts 17:10-12, the Bereans tested everything the apostle Paul said by measuring it against Scripture. And Paul commended them for doing it. Do you think Paul was right or wrong in commending the Berean Christians for testing all things against Scripture?

JEHOVAH'S WITNESS: Well, I guess they were right. But that in itself doesn't take away from the need for the Watchtower Society to instruct Jehovah's people. After all, Jesus himself alluded to the Watchtower Society in the New Testament.

CHRISTIAN: Really? Where did He do that in Scripture?

JEHOVAH'S WITNESS: It's in Matthew 24:45-47. This passage refers to Jehovah's "faithful and discreet slave," which is Christ's 144,000 anointed followers viewed as a group or as an organization, headed by the governing body of the Watchtower Society. Churches and ministries affiliated with apostate Christendom are pictured as the evil slave in this passage.

CHRISTIAN: Where in the text of Matthew's gospel is the Watchtower Society explicitly mentioned?

JEHOVAH'S WITNESS: It's not mentioned directly, but it seems clear that Jesus was referring to the Watchtower Society.

CHRISTIAN: How do you know that?

JEHOVAH'S WITNESS: Well, it's just obvious.

CHRISTIAN: Would it be fair for me to say it was the Watchtower Society who told you Jesus was talking about the Watchtower Society?

JEHOVAH'S WITNESS: That's true.

CHRISTIAN: Do you think a person reading straight through Matthew's Gospel without Watchtower literature would ever arrive at the conclusion that this passage is referring to the Watchtower Society?

JEHOVAH'S WITNESS: Maybe not. But that's one of the reasons Jehovah established the Watchtower Society on earth. It's His mouthpiece to guide people in properly understanding the Scriptures. Without the Watchtower Society people simply cannot understand the Scriptures.

CHRISTIAN: From a plain reading of Matthew 24:45-47, it seems to me that Jesus is simply contrasting faithful and unfaithful followers. He portrays the faithful servant as one who seeks to please his master by doing all the things his master requested. By contrast, the unfaithful servant lives it up while his master is away and doesn't do what his master instructed him to do. Jesus is urging His followers to be faithful and committed. I don't see any allusion to an organization, such as the Watchtower Society, in this passage. While we're on the topic, though, can I ask you another question? When did the Watchtower Society come into being?

JEHOVAH'S WITNESS: In the late nineteenth century.

CHRISTIAN: This makes me wonder…if the Watchtower Society came into being in the late nineteenth century, and if a person cannot understand the Scriptures without the help of the Watchtower Society, then what is that saying about all the people who lived prior to the late nineteenth century? Did none of them understand the Scriptures? And if none of them understood the Scriptures, were none of them saved?

JEHOVAH'S WITNESS: Hmm…I've never been asked that. I'll have to think about it. But off the top of my head, I'd have to say that Scripture does indicate there would be a great deal of apostasy in the world.

CHRISTIAN: I grant you that. But my question remains. If you are correct about the need for the Watchtower Society, then this would seem to spell doom for all the people who lived prior to the late nineteenth century. Also, this makes me wonder about God Himself. If God set up the Watchtower Society in the late nineteenth century, and a person cannot understand the Scriptures without the Watchtower Society, then did God not care about the people who lived prior to this time? Can you help me to understand?

JEHOVAH'S WITNESS: Well, I think He cares. But like I said, I'm going to have to think about this. Did you know that Isaiah 43:10 specifically mentions the witnesses of Jehovah?

CHRISTIAN: Let's take a look. In my Bible it says, "'You are my witnesses,' declares the LORD, 'and my servant whom I have chosen, that you may know and believe me and understand that I am he. Before me no god was formed, nor shall there be any after me.'" So, let me get this straight. You think this verse is referring to the Jehovah's Witnesses, which came into being in the late nineteenth century?

JEHOVAH'S WITNESS: Yes.

CHRISTIAN: In context, though, God is speaking to the Jewish people, who already existed. The verse points to Israel as God's witness to the pagan nations. Can you give me a reason for rejecting this Jewish context? Why would you say this refers to a modern-day religious group that was formed many centuries after God spoke the words?

JEHOVAH'S WITNESS: That's our belief.

CHRISTIAN: It was the Watchtower that taught you that this verse refers to the Watchtower, right?

JEHOVAH'S WITNESS: Yes.

CHRISTIAN: [Smile.] I just can't get away from this nagging question. Were there no witnesses of God prior to the late nineteenth century? Didn't God care about all those people who lived prior to this time?

JEHOVAH'S WITNESS: I think He cared. But I need to give that some further thought.

CHRISTIAN: Speaking of witnesses, would you agree that the disciples in the New Testament were witnesses of Jesus Christ?

JEHOVAH'S WITNESS: We are called to be witnesses of Jehovah.

CHRISTIAN: In Acts 1:8 Jesus instructed His followers, "You will receive power when the Holy Spirit has come upon you, and you will be my witnesses in Jerusalem and in all Judea and Samaria, and to the end of the earth." According to this verse, aren't we to be witnesses of Jesus?

JEHOVAH'S WITNESS: Well, Jesus was a servant of Jehovah. We are ultimately called to be witnesses of Jehovah.

CHRISTIAN: Was Jesus wrong in His instruction in Acts 1:8 that we are to be His witnesses?

JEHOVAH'S WITNESS: I guess not. At least the Jehovah's Witnesses are faithful in being witnesses throughout the world. Unlike other so-called Christian groups, we visit people door to door, as Scripture instructs.

CHRISTIAN: What verse are you thinking of regarding witnessing door to door?

JEHOVAH'S WITNESS: Acts 20:20 in the New World Translation quotes Paul as saying, "I did not hold back from telling you any of the things that were profitable nor from teaching you publicly and from house to house."

CHRISTIAN: So, you think house-to-house witnessing is a sign of God's true people?

JEHOVAH'S WITNESS: Yes. This is unlike today's religious clergy, which forces people to come to them to hear teaching.

CHRISTIAN: What about the Mormons? They do house-to-house witnessing as well. Are they the true people of God?

JEHOVAH'S WITNESS: Well, no. The Jehovah's Witnesses go door to door teaching the truth, not falsehood.

CHRISTIAN: Don't you go to the Kingdom Hall to receive teaching? Why criticize Christians for going to church to receive teaching?

JEHOVAH'S WITNESS: Fair enough. But Jehovah's Witnesses also teach door to door.

CHRISTIAN: I can't help but think that you might be unaware of the cultural backdrop of Acts 20:20.

JEHOVAH'S WITNESS: How so?

CHRISTIAN: Back in New Testament times, all the churches met in homes. There were no centralized church buildings in those early days of Christianity. Instead there were many house-churches scattered throughout the city. For example, one church met in the house of Mary, the mother of Mark. We see that in Acts 12:12. We also see this in other verses, like Colossians 4:15, Romans 16:5, and 1 Corinthians 16:19.

JEHOVAH'S WITNESS: Okay. And your point is…

CHRISTIAN: It appears that the apostle Paul was going from house-church to house-church. Acts 20:17 even tells us that Paul was addressing church elders within these house-churches. This being so, is it legitimate to take a verse dealing with an apostle visiting churches and extrapolating that all believers today must witness from house to house?

JEHOVAH'S WITNESS: Well, I hadn't thought about that.

CHRISTIAN: Okay. Well, I've enjoyed speaking with you. Before you leave, let me ask you one more thing. Have you ever read the entire Bible alone, without Watchtower literature or any other literature?

JEHOVAH'S WITNESS: I can't say that I have.

CHRISTIAN: Here's a suggestion. Read the Bible alone, all by itself. I urge you to read through the Gospels from either the English Standard Version, the New American Standard Version, the New International Version, or the New Living Translation. I've done a lot of study, and I can assure you that these are really good translations. If you are able to do that, I'd love to get your reaction the next time you stop by. As well, if you like, we can chat about the New World Translation.

JEHOVAH'S WITNESS: I'll think about it.

CHRISTIAN: [Reach out to shake hands.]

Conversation Highlights

In closing, allow me to highlight some tactical points from this conversation.

- At the outset, I silently prayed that God would open the Jehovah's Witness's heart to the truth, just as He did for Lydia in Acts 16:14.

- I was friendly and smiled a lot throughout the entire conversation.

- I listened courteously and never interrupted.

- I agreed with comments when I could.

- I always asked for scriptural support when doctrinal assertions were made.

- I repeated questions when there were evasions.

- I asked questions that clarified facts, shifted the burden of proof, and guided the direction of the conversation.

- My goal was not necessarily to force the Jehovah's Witness to immediately admit the error of all his false assertions. Rather, I made a series of strong points that will stick with him long after he leaves my house.

- I opened the door for another visit.

Digging Deeper

You may be interested in more in-depth information on the Jehovah's Witnesses' view of the Watchtower Society and the specific Bible verses they cite in support. If so, I invite you to consult my book *Reasoning from the Scriptures with the Jehovah's Witnesses* (2009 edition), pages 23–48.

9

Conversations About the New World Translation

———⊶∞∾⊷———

The New World Translation is the Bible that Jehovah's Witnesses use. It was produced and published during the Watchtower presidency of Nathan Knorr (1942–1977). The unique feature of this Bible is that it claims to restore God's name, Jehovah. More specifically, "Jehovah" is inserted in the Old Testament where the Hebrew consonants YHWH appear and in the New Testament where the text refers to the Father—some 237 times in the New Testament despite the fact that not a single Greek manuscript supports this insertion. The Watchtower Society presently publishes some three million New World Translation Bibles per month.[1]

The average Jehovah's Witness who stops by your house trusts this Bible without reserve. He or she probably has no idea that multiple groundless insertions have been made throughout it. Nor is he or she aware of how doctrinally biased (in a cultic way) this translation is. (For example, the wordings in the New World Translation tend to mask the absolute deity of Jesus Christ in keeping with Watchtower theology.) From the average Jehovah's Witness's perspective, the New World Translation is simply the best Bible translation in the world. Jehovah's Witnesses claim that because they are the only group in the world that consistently refers to God by His correct name (Jehovah) and has a Bible that honors God's correct name, they alone are Jehovah's true followers.

The Watchtower Society has always resisted efforts to identify members of the translation committee. The claim was that they preferred to remain anonymous and humble, giving God the glory for this translation. However, such anonymity also served to prevent legitimate biblical scholars from checking their linguistic credentials.

After Raymond Franz defected from the governing body of the Watchtower Society, he wrote a book in which he revealed the identity of the translators—Nathan Knorr, Frederick Franz, Albert Schroeder, George Gangas, and Milton Henschel.[2] It was no longer a secret that the translation committee was completely unqualified for the task. Four of the five men in the committee had no Hebrew or Greek training whatsoever (they had only a high school education). The fifth—Frederick Franz—claimed to know Hebrew and Greek, but upon examination under oath in a court of law in Edinburgh, Scotland, was found to fail a simple Hebrew test.[3]

Falsehoods to Watch For

- In the New World Translation, God's name, Jehovah, has been "faithfully restored" throughout both the Old and New Testaments.

- The New World Translation is the best Bible translation in the world. All other translations are untrustworthy.

- Because Jehovah's Witnesses are the only people on earth to consistently use God's proper name (including in the New World Translation), they alone are Jehovah's true followers.

Important Points to Introduce

- The translators of the New World Translation were not biblical linguists and were completely unqualified for the task.

- Reliable biblical linguists consistently give "two thumbs down" to the New World Translation.

- The New World Translation has undergone major changes through the years.

- The New World Translation mistranslates verses with a view to supporting Watchtower theology.

Eavesdropping on a Conversation

Notice how I transition in this conversation from a topic of lesser importance to a topic of greater importance—in this case, the unreliability of the New World Translation.

JEHOVAH'S WITNESS: Good morning. Do you have a few minutes to chat?

CHRISTIAN: Okay. [Silently pray the open-the-heart prayer.]

JEHOVAH'S WITNESS: There sure is a lot of war today all over the world. It's amazing that even many so-called Christians participate in these wars. Does it ever bother you that people who call themselves Christians are involved in killing other people?

CHRISTIAN: Well, no Christian likes war, but war is sometimes a necessary evil.

JEHOVAH'S WITNESS: Many within Protestant and Catholic churches have participated in war. They do this despite the fact that Christ tells us to love our enemies. How can one claim to love his enemy and yet kill him? The Jehovah's Witnesses are really the only ones who refuse to participate in any wars.

CHRISTIAN: So you're a Jehovah's Witness?

JEHOVAH'S WITNESS: Yes.

CHRISTIAN: I don't know if you're aware of this, but certain Christian denominations also refuse participation in war. Even before the Jehovah's Witnesses came into existence in the late nineteenth century, groups like the Mennonites and Quakers refused participation in war.

JEHOVAH'S WITNESS: Even so, the Jehovah's Witnesses today are one of the most vocal groups to oppose war in obedience to Jehovah. Most Christian groups today—Protestants and Catholics—are disobedient to Jehovah.

CHRISTIAN: That's an interesting claim. Let me ask you this. If refusing to participate in war is a sign of being in the truth as a religious group, would you say that the Mennonites and Quakers are in the truth?

JEHOVAH'S WITNESS: Well, no, because there are other issues to consider as well.

CHRISTIAN: But you would say that a group that is open to war is going against Jehovah's will?

JEHOVAH'S WITNESS: Yes.

CHRISTIAN: No exceptions?

JEHOVAH'S WITNESS: No.

CHRISTIAN: Were you aware that prior to 1939, the Watchtower Society itself allowed participation in war for some sixty years? Was the Watchtower Society going against the will of Jehovah for all that time?

JEHOVAH'S WITNESS: I don't think you are correct in what you said about the Watchtower Society.

CHRISTIAN: I can understand why you would be resistant to my statement. You can confirm what I've said by consulting some of the older Watchtower publications at your Kingdom Hall. [Smile.] Are you up for a homework assignment this week? Maybe not. But if you don't want to research the documentation, I'd be happy to do it for you. Do you want me to?[4]

JEHOVAH'S WITNESS: That won't be necessary.

CHRISTIAN: Okay. But please allow me to make a quick clarification. Even within the various Protestant and Catholic denominations, Christians hold to different views on war. Some are activists. Some are pacifists. And some are selectivists. Do you know what I mean by those terms?

JEHOVAH'S WITNESS: I'm not quite sure.

CHRISTIAN: Okay. Well, activism is the view that Christians should participate in all wars in obedience to their government. They cite Bible passages in which God commands Christians to obey the government, such as Romans 13. Pacifism is the idea that it is always wrong to injure or kill other humans, regardless of the circumstances. They note that Jesus said we are to love our enemies. They also note God's commandments against murder. Selectivism is the view that says Christians are permitted to participate only in just wars, not in unjust wars. These note that even God is called the Lord of Hosts (or Lord of Armies) and that He even commanded the Israelites to engage in wars against pagan nations. I could say a lot more on all this, but my point is that Protestants and Catholics have different views on this issue.

JEHOVAH'S WITNESS: Okay, I can understand that.

CHRISTIAN: Good. It's admittedly a very difficult issue. Even though Christians have different views about it, all Christians cite many Scripture verses to support their views. All Christians, regardless of their view on war, seek to honor God by a correct interpretation of Scripture.

JEHOVAH'S WITNESS: I understand what you're saying. As Jehovah's Witnesses, we believe Scripture teaches that only the Creator has the prerogative of taking the life of one of His creatures.

CHRISTIAN: And you believe Jehovah is the Creator?

JEHOVAH'S WITNESS: Yes.

CHRISTIAN: What about Jesus? Is He the Creator too?

JEHOVAH'S WITNESS: We believe that Jehovah is the primary Creator. Jehovah created Jesus first, as the archangel Michael, and then God used Jesus (or Michael) to create all other things in the universe.

CHRISTIAN: May I ask what made you come to that conclusion?

JEHOVAH'S WITNESS: Well, that's what Scripture says.

CHRISTIAN: Where so?

JEHOVAH'S WITNESS: In Colossians 1:16-17. In the New World Translation we read, "By means of him all [other] things were created in the heavens and upon the earth, the things visible and the things invisible, no matter whether they are thrones or lordships or governments or authorities. All [other] things have been created through him and for him. Also, he is before all [other] things and by means of him all [other] things were made to exist."

CHRISTIAN: You're probably aware that the New World Translation is the only Bible translation that inserts the word "other" four times in these two verses. I've heard Bible scholars say that the word "other" is not in the original Greek text of these verses. Why does the Watchtower Society add to the Word of God?

JEHOVAH'S WITNESS: Well, it's not adding to the Word of God. Sometimes words are inserted with brackets to make for smoother reading.

CHRISTIAN: [Smile.] But doesn't the Watchtower say that words with brackets are inserted into the text only when those insertions do not change the meaning of the text?

JEHOVAH'S WITNESS: Well, yes.

CHRISTIAN: Don't you think the insertion of "other" four times in Colossians 1:16-17 changes the meaning of the text? Instead of saying that Jesus created all things, Jesus is portrayed as creating all other things, as if He himself were a created being. That seems like a pretty big change of meaning.

JEHOVAH'S WITNESS: Well, it clarifies the correct meaning in a smooth way.

CHRISTIAN: But here's the thing I'm struggling with. Perhaps you can help me. Prior to the Watchtower's publication of the New World Translation, Jehovah's Witnesses already believed that Jesus was a created being whom Jehovah used to create all other things. Then, when the New World Translation was produced, these insertions were made to reflect that theological view. Do you think human beings have the prerogative to change God's Word like that?

JEHOVAH'S WITNESS: Well, again, it's not changing God's Word. The use of brackets shows that these words are not actually in God's Word but are only added to make for smoother reading.

CHRISTIAN: I understand. Still, the Watchtower says that such insertions can be made only if they don't change the meaning of the text. But in Colossians 1:16-17 the insertions do change the meaning of the text.

JEHOVAH'S WITNESS: Well, again, it just makes for smoother reading.

CHRISTIAN: I've actually done some study on this and discovered that in the 1950 edition of the New World Translation, the word "other" was inserted four times in Colossians 1:16-17 without any brackets at all. This made it appear that these words were actually God's Word. It wasn't until biblical linguists exposed all this publicly that the Watchtower inserted brackets in subsequent editions. Do you see anything wrong with the Watchtower's handling of all this?

JEHOVAH'S WITNESS: Well, I'm sure there was no intentional wrong. The words help to clarify the meaning and make for smoother reading.

CHRISTIAN: Did you know that Scripture itself warns against adding to or taking away from God's Word? Revelation 22:18-19 says, "I warn everyone who hears the words of the prophecy of this book: if anyone adds to them, God will add to him the plagues described in this book, and if anyone takes away from the words of the book of this prophecy, God will take away his share in the tree of life and in the holy city, which are described in this book." Deuteronomy 4:2 says, "You shall not add to the word that I command you, nor take from it." Proverbs 30:6 warns, "Do not add to his words." In view of these verses, do you personally feel completely comfortable with the Watchtower's insertion of the word "other" four times in Colossians 1:16-17?

JEHOVAH'S WITNESS: Well, you need to keep in mind that the Watchtower Society is the mouthpiece of Jehovah on earth. It speaks for Jehovah.

CHRISTIAN: Are you saying that Jehovah commands the Watchtower Society to do what He has elsewhere forbidden in the pages of Scripture? Does Jehovah contradict himself?

JEHOVAH'S WITNESS: No, but you can trust the New World Translation because it comes from Jehovah's mouthpiece on earth.

CHRISTIAN: Did you know that the Watchtower Society's own Greek interlinear version of the Bible says the Greek word in these verses means "all things," not "all other things"?

JEHOVAH'S WITNESS: No. I'll have to check that out.

CHRISTIAN: [Smile.] Here's something else I've discovered. In Isaiah 44:24, God (or Jehovah) says to His people, "I am the LORD, who made all things, who alone stretched out the heavens, who spread out the earth by myself." Here's my question. If God is the one who alone created the universe by Himself, and if Jesus is the Creator as Colossians 1:16 indicates, then doesn't this show that Jesus Himself is absolute deity?

JEHOVAH'S WITNESS: Well, Jehovah alone did create the universe, but He did so through the instrument of Jesus, who was created first.

CHRISTIAN: But Isaiah 44:24 says that Jehovah created the universe alone. He says, "By myself."

JEHOVAH'S WITNESS: Jehovah alone did it through Jesus.

CHRISTIAN: [Smile.] John 1:3 says of Jesus, "All things were made through him, and without him was not any thing made that was made." If Jesus created all things as John 1:3 says, and if only Jehovah is the Creator as Isaiah 44:24 affirms, then doesn't this point to the absolute deity of Jesus Christ?

JEHOVAH'S WITNESS: We believe Jesus is a lesser god through whom Jehovah created the universe. That's why the Watchtower worded Colossians 1:16 the way it did.

CHRISTIAN: [With genuine concern:] I know that as a Jehovah's Witness you are not supposed to question the Watchtower Society. I understand that, and I'm sympathetic to how difficult it may be to hear all this. But if the Watchtower Society changes God's Word—and if God's Word itself condemns all who seek to change it—then do you really want to be affiliated with this organization?

JEHOVAH'S WITNESS: The organization speaks for Jehovah.

CHRISTIAN: It is now widely known that the translators of the New World Translation were Nathan Knorr, Frederick Franz, Albert Schroeder, George Gangas, and Milton Henschel. Did you know that none of these individuals were trained in biblical Hebrew or Greek? If a Bible is translated by people who do not know the original languages, is that a translation a person should trust?

JEHOVAH'S WITNESS: Well, I think Jehovah speaks through the Watchtower Society, so He guided the translation.

CHRISTIAN: I understand your view. But if Jehovah guided the New World Translation, how can we explain the major changes that have been made in it through the years? For example, the 1961 edition of the New World Translation supported the worship of Jesus. Hebrews 1:6 was translated, "But when he again brings his first-born into the inhabited earth, he says: 'And let all God's angels worship him.'" Later, the Watchtower Society changed its mind on worshipping Jesus. The 1971 edition of the New World Translation reads, "But when he again brings his Firstborn into the inhabited earth, he says: 'And let all God's angels do obeisance to him.'" Why was this change made? Does it mean Jehovah didn't effectively guide or oversee the New World Translation for its 1961 edition?

JEHOVAH'S WITNESS: I haven't heard of that before. I'll have to look into it.

CHRISTIAN: All this is in keeping with changes we see in *The Watchtower* magazine. Early issues of the magazine—back in the late 1800s—said we should worship Jesus. By 1964, *Watchtower* magazines said that worship of Jesus was "unscriptural." That makes me ask, is this really an organization you want to trust in regard to your eternal salvation?

JEHOVAH'S WITNESS: There may be changes, but that's because new light has been received from Jehovah.

CHRISTIAN: Okay. Does that mean new light from Jehovah can contradict old light from Jehovah?

JEHOVAH'S WITNESS: The light is much brighter today than it was in years past.

CHRISTIAN: What if forty years from now, the light gets so bright that you discover that most of what you currently believe is incorrect? And what if you die tomorrow? What if after you die, new light emerges that indicates you never knew the truth? Do you really want to trust an organization that has those kinds of "new light" loopholes?

JEHOVAH'S WITNESS: Well, I'm not sure what to say about that.

CHRISTIAN: [With genuine concern:] I'd love to talk some more with you about all this. But here's one final thing I want to leave with you. The Watchtower Society claims to have restored the name of Jehovah throughout both the Old and New Testaments. In the New Testament alone, the word Jehovah has been inserted 237 times where the text is believed to refer to the Father. The truth is, the word Jehovah is not found in any legitimate New Testament Greek manuscripts. This is another example of the Watchtower Society changing the Word of God, which is something that God condemns. I really encourage you to read straight through the New Testament using a reliable Bible translation, such as the English Standard Version, the New American Standard Bible, the New International Version, or the New Living Translation. If you do, you will be stunned to discover that the Bible truly is a Jesus book. Would you be willing to do that? And can we set a date and topic for our next meeting?

Conversation Highlights

Allow me to highlight a few tactical points from this conversation.

- I redirected the conversation from their chosen topic (war) to the more significant issue of the unreliability of the New World Translation.

- I seized every opportunity available to kindly but firmly highlight problems with the Watchtower Society (for example, its doctrinal changes).

- I kindly raised the issue of changes in the New World Translation, thus further challenging the trustworthiness of the Watchtower Society.

- In a kind but persistent way, I stated and restated how the Watchtower Society has changed the Word of God.

- I requested a date for the next visit. I also asked about setting the topic. That way, I can prepare well for our next meeting.

Digging Deeper

You may be interested in more in-depth information on the Jehovah's Witnesses' view of the New World Translation. If so, I invite you to consult my book *Reasoning from the Scriptures with the Jehovah's Witnesses* (2009 edition), pages 69–98.

10

Conversations About Jehovah

⸺◦∞◦⸺

Jehovah's Witnesses consistently refer to God by the name of Jehovah. They believe using the name Jehovah is critically important when referring to God, and they cite supporting verses from the New World Translation. For example, they cite Exodus 3:15, which tells us that Jehovah is God's name "to time indefinite." This means that God's name will never change, they say. Jehovah was God's name in biblical times, and Jehovah is God's name today. The Watchtower book *Let Your Name Be Sanctified* explains it this way:

> To this very generation in the twentieth century...the name of the eternal God is JEHOVAH. To all eternity this is his holy name, and, as the memorial of him, it is the name by which we are to remember him to all eternity. It is his unchangeable name. From the beginning of man's existence to Moses' day it had not changed; and from Moses back there in 1514 B.C.E. till today that name has not changed. So after all these thousands of years of time it is fitting for us to use that name in a worthy way.[1]

Jehovah's Witnesses also point to the necessity of using God's correct name in relation to salvation. Romans 10:13 in the New World Translation reads, "Everyone who calls on the name of Jehovah will be saved."

As might be expected, Jehovah's Witnesses make quite an impression on the doorstep when they inform the unwary and biblically illiterate person (including some Christians) that the proper use of God's correct name (Jehovah) is absolutely essential to one's salvation. When they combine that claim with their claim that they are the only religious group on earth to consistently refer to God by the name Jehovah, they are able to convince many that they are the only true followers of God. Baptists, Presbyterians, Methodists, and other denominations of Christianity are supposedly included in the false apostate church, whose doctrines are inspired by the devil.

I will talk about Jesus more fully in other chapters, but it is important to note here the Watchtower claim that Jesus is not Jehovah. "If Jesus of the 'New Testament' is Jehovah of the 'Old Testament,' as many claim, should there not at least be one biblical reference saying that Jesus is Jehovah? Yet there is not one."[2] Rather, they say, Jesus was created as the archangel Michael. "There is Scriptural evidence for concluding that Michael was the name of Jesus Christ before he left heaven and after his return."[3] "Michael the great prince is none other than Jesus Christ himself."[4]

Falsehoods to Watch For

- God's only true name is Jehovah.
- The use of the name Jehovah is essential to salvation.
- Jesus is not Jehovah.
- Because the various denominations of Christianity do not consistently use the name Jehovah, they are false churches that have been influenced by the devil.

Important Points to Introduce

- Jehovah is not God's only name.
- People created the name Jehovah by combining consonants of YHWH and vowels of Adonai.
- God has other names besides Jehovah, including *Yahweh-Nissi* ("the Lord our banner"), *Elohim* ("strong one"), *El Shaddai* ("mighty God who is compassionate"), *Adonai*

("Lord," "Master"), *Lord of hosts* (commander of the
angelic army), and many others.

- Jesus never referred to the Father as Jehovah in the New
  Testament.

- Believers are uniquely privileged to call God "Father."

- Salvation does not depend on the use of the name Jehovah.

- The New Testament consistently uplifts Jesus.

- Jesus is Jehovah (or Yahweh).

Eavesdropping on a Conversation

Notice how I transition in this conversation from a topic of lesser
importance to a topic of greater importance—in this case, God's name
Jehovah.

JEHOVAH'S WITNESS: Good morning. My colleague and I are Jehovah's Witnesses, and we're visiting your neighborhood today.
Would you mind if we chat for a few minutes?

CHRISTIAN: I guess that'd be okay. [Silently pray the open-the-heart
prayer.]

JEHOVAH'S WITNESS: Great. I wanted to ask you if you're aware that
many of the holidays celebrated by Christians are actually pagan
holidays? I'm talking about holidays like Christmas and Easter.

CHRISTIAN: What made you come to that conclusion?

JEHOVAH'S WITNESS: Well, let's take Christmas as an example. Recognized authorities tell us that Christ was not even born on December
25. The truth is, December 25 is the day the ancient Babylonians
celebrated a pagan holiday. Apparently, paganism made its way
into the early church with the celebration of Christmas.

CHRISTIAN: Are you saying that any Christian group that celebrates
Christmas is influenced by paganism?

JEHOVAH'S WITNESS: It's a legitimate concern. The Jehovah's Witnesses
are the only Christian group that doesn't celebrate such holidays. The
Jehovah's Witnesses refuse to be influenced by any form of paganism.

CHRISTIAN: I'm a little confused. Perhaps you can help me. I wonder if you're aware that the Watchtower Society once celebrated these so-called pagan holidays?

JEHOVAH'S WITNESS: Sounds like you *are* a little confused!

CHRISTIAN: [Smile.] Well, I've actually studied this issue. Sixty years after the Watchtower was founded, they changed their policy on these holidays. Until then, Jehovah's Witnesses celebrated Christmas and Easter annually. In view of what you said earlier, does this mean that the Watchtower Society was once pagan-influenced?

JEHOVAH'S WITNESS: I don't think you've got your facts right on this.

CHRISTIAN: [Smile.] Are you open to a little homework assignment this week? Maybe over the next week you can check out some old Watchtower publications at your Kingdom Hall. If you have any problems finding those references to Christmas, I'd be happy to pitch in and find the documentation for you. Are you game?[5]

JEHOVAH'S WITNESS: That won't be necessary at this point. Even aside from the holiday issue, there are other clear signs of pagan influence in the church, such as the pagan doctrine of the Trinity.

CHRISTIAN: I've love to chat about the Trinity with you a bit later, but I'm still very interested in our discussion about Christmas. From what I understand, the early Christians refused to participate in the holiday celebrated by Babylonian pagans on December 25. Their reasoning was that if these pagans were going to celebrate pagan deities on December 25, Christians would counter by celebrating the true Messiah on the same day. Seen in that light, celebrating Christmas isn't pagan, is it?

JEHOVAH'S WITNESS: Do you think Christmas as it is celebrated today honors Jehovah?

CHRISTIAN: Well, that's an interesting question that calls for a balanced answer. On the one hand, I think it's great for Christians to celebrate the birth of Jesus the Messiah. They do so only because they love Him. On the other hand, I'd be the first to agree that the crass materialism that many people make of Christmas is not a good thing.

JEHOVAH'S WITNESS: Well, we at least agree on something.

CHRISTIAN: [Smile.] Say, something you said earlier sparked my interest. You said you are a Jehovah's Witness. Why does your group place such a heavy emphasis on the name Jehovah?

JEHOVAH'S WITNESS: Scripture tells us that the name Jehovah is the name by which God is to be known for all generations.

CHRISTIAN: What verse is that?

JEHOVAH'S WITNESS: Exodus 3:15 in the New World Translation reads, "This is what you are to say to the sons of Israel, 'Jehovah the God of your forefathers, the God of Abraham, the God of Isaac and the God of Jacob, has sent me to you.' This is my name to time indefinite, and this is the memorial of me to generation after generation." So, Jehovah is God's name for all eternity.

CHRISTIAN: But God isn't only called Jehovah in Scripture, right? Sometimes the Old Testament refers to God as "the God of Abraham, the God of Isaac, and the God of Jacob." And sometimes He is called "the Lord of hosts." There are also many compound names used of God in the Bible.

JEHOVAH'S WITNESS: What do you mean?

CHRISTIAN: Well, compound names join two names together, and they always communicate something important about God. For example, God is called *Yahweh Raah* in Psalm 23:1. This name means "the Lord our shepherd." God is called *Yahweh Rapha* in Exodus 15:26. This name means "the Lord who heals."

JEHOVAH'S WITNESS: Okay.

CHRISTIAN: So in view of this, you wouldn't say that Jehovah is the *only* name by which God can be known, right?

JEHOVAH'S WITNESS: Well, Exodus 3:15 says that Jehovah is God's name for all eternity.

CHRISTIAN: I understand. But my point is that Jehovah is not the only name by which God can be called. In the New Testament, Jesus commonly referred to God as "Father," and believers address Him as "Father" as well. In fact, since believers are God's children, they are uniquely privileged to come before the Father and call out to Him, "Abba! Father!" That's in Romans 8:15 and Galatians 4:6. "Abba" is a term of intimacy and affection, loosely carrying the idea of "papa" or "daddy." Do you think of God as your spiritual papa or daddy? Don't you yearn for that type of intimate relationship?

JEHOVAH'S WITNESS: Well, I always think of Him by His eternal name, Jehovah.

CHRISTIAN: I'm aware that your Bible, the New World Translation, uses the name Jehovah all the way through it, including in the New Testament. But can I say something without meaning to sound offensive? There is not a single legitimate Greek New Testament manuscript that includes the term Jehovah. Not one. Certainly I admire your commitment to your beliefs, but since your eternal salvation is at stake, don't you want to make sure that you get this issue right? Don't you want to examine what Scripture itself really teaches about this issue instead of trusting an organization that came into being in the late nineteenth century?

JEHOVAH'S WITNESS: The Watchtower Society is Jehovah's mouthpiece on earth, and it speaks the truth.

CHRISTIAN: Did you know that the word Jehovah is not a biblical name, but is rather a man-made name? The ancient Hebrew manuscripts refer to YHWH. The original Hebrew had only consonants. Most scholars today render it Yahweh. The term Yahweh is loaded with meaning, for it carries the idea of self-existence. Yahweh is the eternal one. God's desire was for every generation to recognize that He is truly the self-existent and eternal one, as contrasted with temporal pagan deities of neighboring nations.

JEHOVAH'S WITNESS: I agree that He is eternal.

CHRISTIAN: Good. [Smile.] But again, the term Jehovah is a man-made term. The ancient Jews developed a superstitious dread of pronouncing the name YHWH. They felt that if they uttered this name, they might violate the third commandment, which deals with taking God's name in vain. This commandment is found in Exodus 20:7. The ancient Jews eventually decided to insert the vowels from Adonai (a-o-a) in the consonants YHWH, resulting in Yahowah, or Jehovah. What it comes down to is this: The name Jehovah is not in the ancient Hebrew manuscripts. YHWH is.

JEHOVAH'S WITNESS: Well, some of the Bibles used by various Christian denominations use the name Jehovah, including the King James Version and the American Standard Version.

CHRISTIAN: Fair enough. You're right that the King James Version uses the name Jehovah, but only in four verses. You're also right that the American Standard Version uses this name.

JEHOVAH'S WITNESS: So you really can't argue against the Watchtower Society for using this name.

CHRISTIAN: I'm glad you raised that point. The truth is, Bible scholars are unsure how to pronounce YHWH. I think the scholars who render it as Yahweh are right. But some have opted for Jehovah. Personally, I don't criticize the Watchtower Society for using the name Jehovah where YHWH appears in the Hebrew manuscripts. But I do think the Watchtower Society is wrong to have inserted the name hundreds of times in the New Testament when there is not a single legitimate New Testament Greek manuscript that supports it. [With genuine concern:] I hate to say it, but the Watchtower Society has changed the Word of God.

JEHOVAH'S WITNESS: I'm not sure you're correct about the New Testament. I'll have to check that out.

CHRISTIAN: [Smile.] I encourage you to. A good example of what I'm talking about is Romans 10:13, where we read in the New World Translation, "Everyone who calls on the name of Jehovah will be saved." This makes it appear that a person cannot be saved without using the name Jehovah. The problem is, there's no legitimate New Testament Greek manuscript that has the name Jehovah here. The verse actually reads, "Everyone who calls on the name of the Lord will be saved." And if you look at verses 9 through 13, the term "Lord" is clearly referring to Jesus Christ. We are to call upon the Lord Jesus for salvation.

JEHOVAH'S WITNESS: Hmm…I haven't heard that before. I'll have to look into that further.

CHRISTIAN: Good. I hope you do because this is a salvation issue. I know you want to make sure you're saved, so definitely do your research on this one. I'm happy to help you do it if you like.

JEHOVAH'S WITNESS: That won't be necessary at this point.

CHRISTIAN: Okay. There's an important qualification I want to mention to you. Romans 10:13 is actually a quote or allusion to Joel 2:32, which refers to calling upon YHWH for salvation. But this does not justify using the term Jehovah in Romans 10:13. The only reason I'm pointing this out to you is that calling upon Yahweh in Joel 2:32 is equated with calling upon Jesus in Romans 10:13, thereby proving the absolute deity of Jesus Christ. We are saved by calling upon Jesus.

JEHOVAH'S WITNESS: Okay. Well, I'll give that some thought. I need to be leaving.

CHRISTIAN: [Smile.] Okay. I'd love to talk more about Jesus the next time you stop by. Let me at least leave this with you. There is a prophecy in the Old Testament that speaks about how John the Baptist would prepare for the coming of Jesus Christ. It is found in Isaiah 40:3, and it reads, "A voice cries: 'In the wilderness prepare the way of the LORD; make straight in the desert a highway for our God.'" The divine names Yahweh and Elohim are both used in this verse. It literally says, "A voice cries: 'In the wilderness prepare the way of the LORD [Yahweh]; make straight in the desert a highway for our God [Elohim].'" Mark 1:2-4 says this verse was fulfilled in John the Baptist preparing the way for the coming of Jesus Christ. Jesus is clearly Yahweh and Elohim. Can we set a date so we can talk more about Jesus?

Conversation Highlights

Allow me to highlight a few tactical points from this conversation.

- I transitioned from their chosen topic of Christmas to the more important topic of the name Jehovah.
- To avoid appearing rude, I did not transition immediately. I discussed Christmas for a few minutes first.

- When the Jehovah's Witness felt like he was running out of steam on his Christmas argument, he tried to switch to talking about the Trinity. I kindly redirected the subject back onto Christmas.

- I offered to help find documentation regarding the assertions I made about the Watchtower Society. This added credibility to the assertions.

- I challenged the trustworthiness of the Watchtower Society by revealing some of its changes to the Word of God.

- I purposefully sought to exalt Jesus in this discussion about Jehovah.

- I showed that Christians can call God "Abba," meaning "papa" or "daddy." The Jehovah's Witness lacks this sense of intimacy with Jehovah but inwardly craves it.

- Throughout, I spoke the truth in love (see Ephesians 4:15).

Digging Deeper

You may be interested in more in-depth information on the Jehovah's Witnesses' view of the divine name and the specific Bible verses they cite to support it. If so, I invite you to consult my book *Reasoning from the Scriptures with the Jehovah's Witnesses* (2009 edition), pages 49–68.

11

Conversations About Jesus and the Archangel Michael

—— ∞ ——

The Watchtower Society teaches that Jesus was originally created as the archangel Michael.[1] The Watchtower book *Reasoning from the Scriptures* tells us, "The evidence indicates that the Son of God was known as Michael before he came to earth and is known also by that name since his return to heaven where he resides as the glorified spirit Son of God."[2] We are assured that "'Michael the great prince' is none other than Jesus Christ himself."[3]

Though Michael (Jesus) existed in his prehuman state as an angel for billions of years, at the appointed time he was born on earth as a human being—ceasing his existence as an angel. In order to ransom humankind from sin, Michael gave up his existence as a spirit creature (angel) when his life force was transferred into Mary's womb by Jehovah. This was not an Incarnation (God in the flesh). Rather, Jesus became a perfect human. He also died as a mere human.

Falsehoods to Watch For

- Jesus is not an eternal being, but rather was created.
- Jesus was created specifically as the archangel Michael.

Important Points to Introduce

- Jesus was not a created being, but rather is eternal.
- Jesus was not Michael the archangel in the Old Testament.

- Jesus Himself created the angels and is worshipped by the angels.

- Michael was merely a prince. Jesus is the King of kings and Lord of lords.

Eavesdropping on a Conversation

Notice how I transition in this conversation from a topic of lesser importance to a topic of greater importance—in this case, debunking the Watchtower view that Jesus is the archangel Michael.

JEHOVAH'S WITNESS: Good morning. My colleague and I are Jehovah's Witnesses, and we're visiting your neighborhood this afternoon. We'd love to briefly chat with you if you have a moment.

CHRISTIAN: Sure, that's fine. [Silently pray the open-the-heart prayer.]

JEHOVAH'S WITNESS: It might interest you to know that through the years, the Jehovah's Witnesses have been growing at a phenomenal pace. Jehovah's blessing on this organization has been pretty amazing.

CHRISTIAN: What made you conclude that rapid growth proves Jehovah's blessing?

JEHOVAH'S WITNESS: It seems pretty obvious, doesn't it?

CHRISTIAN: [Smile.] I can understand why you'd say that. But I'm not sure that the idea holds up to scrutiny. For one thing, other religious groups are far larger than the Jehovah's Witnesses. The Mormons come to mind. They're more than twice the size of the Jehovah's Witnesses. Would you say that the rapid growth of the Mormon church is an indication of Jehovah's blessing on it?

JEHOVAH'S WITNESS: Well, no, because they are not in the truth.

CHRISTIAN: What about Islam, one of the fastest-growing religions in the world? Do you think Islam's growth is an indication of Jehovah's blessing?

JEHOVAH'S WITNESS: Okay, I see your point. But there are many indications beyond sheer growth that point to Jehovah's blessing on the Jehovah's Witnesses.

CHRISTIAN: I don't doubt that you believe that. But this numerical growth point is an important issue. Would you mind if I ask you another question about it?

JEHOVAH'S WITNESS: Not at all.

CHRISTIAN: What about the early days of the Jehovah's Witnesses? I'm referring to the years following the founding of the organization. From my understanding, there wasn't much growth in those early years. In fact, during the Watchtower presidency of Charles Taze Russell, the numbers actually decreased in the organization for a time, right? What do you make of that?

JEHOVAH'S WITNESS: Well, I see your point. But any organization struggles at first.

CHRISTIAN: [Smile.] It seems like the organization has also struggled in recent history. I'm referring to the more than 100,000 Jehovah's Witnesses who left the organization after the Watchtower's 1975 prophecy failed. Did you know that during that year, Jehovah was prophesied to overthrow all human governments and set up His kingdom on earth? In the years preceding that, many Jehovah's Witnesses quit their jobs to witness door to door. Some even used their life savings for this purpose. When the prophecy failed, multitudes of Jehovah's Witnesses left the organization. Have you ever thought about how that might relate to the claim that numerical growth shows Jehovah's blessing?

JEHOVAH'S WITNESS: Well, I think a lot of people misunderstood what the Watchtower Society was saying back then.

CHRISTIAN: Really? *The Watchtower* magazines in the early seventies seem pretty explicit. Have you examined them?

JEHOVAH'S WITNESS: Not specifically.

CHRISTIAN: Would you be willing to examine them?

JEHOVAH'S WITNESS: Maybe.

CHRISTIAN: Good. I'd be happy to help you with the documentation if you like.[4]

JEHOVAH'S WITNESS: Ah…that won't be necessary.

CHRISTIAN: Okay. To tell you the truth, it's not just issues related to prophecy that I'm concerned about. I'm also concerned about the doctrines taught by the Watchtower Society. Doesn't it teach that Jesus was the archangel Michael in Old Testament times?

JEHOVAH'S WITNESS: Yes. And we believe there are good Scriptures to support that idea.

CHRISTIAN: Can you share some of them?

JEHOVAH'S WITNESS: We believe Jesus was the first being in the universe created by Jehovah, and he was created as the archangel Michael. This idea is supported in the book of Daniel. Daniel 10:13 in the New World Translation refers to Michael as "one of the foremost princes." In Daniel 12:1 we are told that "Michael will stand up, the great prince who is standing in behalf of the sons of your people." So prior to Jesus's birth on earth, he was a great prince in his prehuman state. We also believe that at his resurrection, Jesus became Michael again in his posthuman state.

CHRISTIAN: [Smile.] I'm curious. Where do you see any clear indication in Daniel 10 that these references to the archangel Michael relate to Jesus? Is this idea explicitly affirmed anywhere in Daniel 10?

JEHOVAH'S WITNESS: No. But the Watchtower Society has done a lot of study on all this, and these verses shed a great deal of light on Jesus's prehuman state.

CHRISTIAN: Wow, I'm just not seeing it. The verse you quoted calls Michael "one of the foremost princes." Doesn't that indicate that there is more than one foremost prince? It would seem that Michael is portrayed as one among equals. Jesus, by contrast, is portrayed as completely unique in the New Testament. In fact, He is called the King of kings and Lord of lords in Revelation 19:16. A chief prince would have limited authority. But the King of kings and Lord of lords has complete sovereignty. Do you see the distinction?

JEHOVAH'S WITNESS: Hmm...I haven't thought about that before. But perhaps Jesus was a chief prince in Old Testament times and later became more exalted as a king.

CHRISTIAN: The first three chapters of the book of Hebrews establish the superiority of Jesus not only over all human prophets but also over the entire angelic realm. We see that in Hebrews 1:5–2:18. For example, Hebrews 1:5 says that no angel can be called God's Son like Jesus is. Not only that, verse 6 tells us that Christ is worshipped by all the angels.

JEHOVAH'S WITNESS: Well, we think that the angels show obeisance to Jesus, and that's how the New World Translation renders it.

CHRISTIAN: I understand. But I've done some study on this. Did you know that the Greek word translated "worship" in this verse is the exact same Greek word used of worshipping Jehovah? If words mean anything, Jesus was worshipped with the same worship as that shown to Jehovah. And since *all* the angels worship Jesus, that means that He Himself must be completely distinct from the angelic realm.

JEHOVAH'S WITNESS: Hmm…I'll have to think about that.

CHRISTIAN: [Smile.] I'm glad you'll think about it. Here's another thing I've learned. Colossians 1:16 in my Bible says that by Jesus, "all things were created, in heaven and on earth, visible and invisible, whether thrones or dominions or rulers or authorities—all things were created through him and for him." The words thrones, dominions, rulers, and authorities were terms the ancient Jews used to refer to the different orders of angels. So Jesus is the one who created the angels. This means Jesus is in an entirely different class from the angels. He is the Creator; they are among the created.

JEHOVAH'S WITNESS: I haven't heard that before. We believe that Jehovah created Jesus first, and then Jehovah used Jesus to create all other things in the universe.

CHRISTIAN: I understand. That's why the Watchtower Society inserted the word "other" four times in Colossians 1:16-17 in the New World Translation. The word "other" is not in the original Greek text, as the Watchtower's own *Kingdom Interlinear Translation of the Greek Scriptures* demonstrates. But the main thing I want to ask you about relates to Isaiah 44:24, where Jehovah Himself tells His people, "I am the LORD, who made all things, who alone stretched out the heavens, who spread out the earth by myself." Jehovah says He created all things alone and by Himself. If only Jehovah (or Yahweh) is the Creator, and if Jesus is the Creator, this would seem to indicate that Jesus is absolute deity. How do you relate Isaiah 44:24 to Jesus's role in creation?

JEHOVAH'S WITNESS: Jehovah alone created the universe through his junior partner, Jesus, then known as the archangel Michael.

CHRISTIAN: How then could Jehovah say He created the universe alone and by Himself?

JEHOVAH'S WITNESS: Hmm…I'm not sure about that. I'll have to think about it.

CHRISTIAN: Here's another point to consider. Hebrews 2:5 tells us that the world is not (and never will be) subjected to an angel. And yet we are told in Revelation 19:16 that Jesus will reign as King of kings and Lord of lords. Doesn't this seem to argue against the idea that Jesus was the archangel Michael in Old Testament times and became the archangel Michael again at His resurrection? What do you make of Hebrews 2:5?

JEHOVAH'S WITNESS: Hmm…I'll have to check that out. But there's another verse that supports the idea that Jesus was the archangel Michael—1 Thessalonians 4:16. The New World Translation renders this verse, "The Lord himself will descend from heaven with a commanding call, with an archangel's voice and with God's trumpet, and those who are dead in union with Christ will rise first." If the Lord issues his call with an archangel's voice, then he must in fact be the archangel.

CHRISTIAN: I understand why you might reach that conclusion. Personally, I don't think that interpretation holds up to scrutiny. After all, if issuing a call with an archangel's voice makes Jesus an archangel, then by that same logic, wouldn't Jesus's issuing the call "with God's trumpet" mean that he is God?

JEHOVAH'S WITNESS: Hmm…I never noticed that part of the verse. I'd have to give that some thought.

CHRISTIAN: Now, to be clear, I personally don't think that Jesus issuing the call with God's trumpet proves His deity. Many other verses establish His deity very clearly. Likewise, I don't think that Jesus's issuing the call with an archangel's voice means He is the archangel. That's just bad logic.

JEHOVAH'S WITNESS: [A little flustered:] Hmm…

CHRISTIAN: You know what? It just struck me that the "bad logic" barb was rude. I'm sorry about that. I didn't mean to come across that way.

JEHOVAH'S WITNESS: No problem.

CHRISTIAN: Thanks. Can I share another verse with you?

JEHOVAH'S WITNESS: Okay.

CHRISTIAN: Scripture is clear that Michael the archangel does not have the authority to rebuke Satan. We see this in Jude 9. By contrast, Jesus clearly does have the authority to rebuke Satan. For example, when Jesus recognized that Satan was speaking through Peter, Jesus said to him: "Get behind me, Satan." That's in Mark 8:33. Since Michael could not rebuke the devil in his own authority and Jesus could and did, Michael and Jesus cannot be the same person. Is there a flaw in my thinking?

JEHOVAH'S WITNESS: Well, I haven't heard that before. I'll have to think about it.

CHRISTIAN: Notice that when Michael was unable to rebuke Satan, he simply said, "The Lord rebuke you." That's in Jude 9. The word "Lord" is the standard word used throughout the New Testament to refer to Jesus Christ. Michael appealed to Jesus's authority because Michael himself did not have the authority.

JEHOVAH'S WITNESS: Okay…

CHRISTIAN: I want you to notice something else here. If Michael was indeed appealing to the authority of Jesus in this verse, as there is every reason to believe, then Michael and Jesus coexist at the same time, and therefore Jesus could not possibly be Michael.

JEHOVAH'S WITNESS: Okay…well, I'll definitely have to look into that further. I'm not sure how to answer that.

CHRISTIAN: [Smile.] I encourage you to look further into it. Before you leave, though, I want you to know the profound change that the Lord Jesus Christ has brought into my life. The Jesus I worship truly is the King of kings and Lord of lords, and when I became a believer in Him, He not only completely took care of my sin problem but also walks with me through every crisis I face in life. He is my beloved Shepherd. You really don't have to submit to an authoritative organization to be close to Him. Jesus offers you an abundant life, and He offers it today. [Jehovah's Witnesses most often visit in twos, so address the following comment to both.] I want both of you to know that you can come back either as a twosome or individually if you ever want to talk more about Jesus and the salvation He offers you. How about we set a date for our next meeting?

Conversation Highlights

Allow me to highlight a few tactical points from this conversation.

- I thoroughly challenged the claim that rapid growth proves Jehovah's blessing. I took every opportunity I could to challenge the Watchtower Society.

- I transitioned from their chosen topic of the rapid growth rate of the Jehovah's Witnesses to the more important topic of Jesus's identity.

- I offered to provide Watchtower documentation for some of my assertions. That added credibility to my assertions.

- I apologized when I perceived I was rude.

- I offered a brief testimony at the end. Jehovah's Witnesses will always remember your testimony, so feel free to use this approach whenever the opportunity arises.

- I invited one or both to return to talk about Jesus and salvation. If one of them is having secret doubts, I want him or her to feel free to visit me without his or her partner.

Digging Deeper

You may be interested in more in-depth information on the Jehovah's Witnesses' view of Jesus and the archangel Michael and the specific Bible verses they cite to support it. If so, I invite you to consult my book *Reasoning from the Scriptures with the Jehovah's Witnesses* (2009 edition), pages 173–194.

12

Conversations About Jesus and Jehovah

⁓

In Watchtower theology, Jesus is not an eternal being. He was created as the archangel Michael billions of years ago. Then Jehovah used Michael (Jesus) to create all other things in the universe.

Jehovah's Witnesses thus believe in two gods—one is Jehovah, considered to be God Almighty, and the other is Jesus, considered to be a lesser god. To support their claim that Jesus is a lesser god, Jehovah's Witnesses appeal to many verses that supposedly prove that Jesus is inferior to Jehovah. For example, they cite 1 Corinthians 11:3, which tells us that "the head of Christ is God." Jesus is called God's "only begotten Son" (John 3:16 NASB). Jesus is the beginning of Jehovah's creation (Revelation 3:14). Jesus affirmed, "The Father is greater than I" (John 14:28) and referred to the Father as "my God" (John 20:17).

The Watchtower also has a distorted view of the Incarnation. In the biblical view, the Son of God forsook the splendor of heaven and became as genuinely human as we ourselves are, all the while fully retaining His divine nature. To deny either the undiminished deity or the perfect humanity of Christ in the Incarnation is to put oneself outside the pale of orthodoxy. Jesus in the Incarnation was fully human (see Luke 2:40,52; Romans 8:3; Galatians 4:4-5; Philippians 2:5-11; 1 Timothy 3:16; Hebrews 2:14; 1 John 4:2-3) *and* fully God (John 8:58; 10:30; 20:28-29; Colossians 2:9). Though the incarnate Christ had both a human and a divine nature, He was only one person—as indicated by His consistent use of "I," "me," and "mine" in reference to Himself. Jesus never used the words "us," "we," or "ours" when referring to His human-divine person. He was one person with two natures.

Contrary to the biblical view, the Watchtower teaches that in the

Incarnation, an angel became a man. More specifically, at the proper time in Jehovah's timetable, Michael gave up his existence as a spirit creature (angel), and his life force was transferred into Mary's womb by Jehovah. This means that Jesus in the Incarnation was not God in human flesh, but rather just a man.

Accordingly, the Jehovah's Witnesses teach that Jesus was not worshipped in the same sense that the Father (Jehovah) was. The *Watchtower* magazine says, "It is unscriptural for worshippers of the living and true God to render worship to the Son of God, Jesus Christ."[1] Even though the same Greek word used for worshipping Jehovah (*proskuneo*) is used of worshipping Jesus Christ, the Watchtower Society says that the word should be translated "obeisance" and not "worship" when used of Christ.

I will deal with the crucifixion, resurrection, and second coming of Jesus Christ in subsequent chapters. For the sake of continuity and a full understanding, however, I will briefly summarize the Watchtower view.

In the Incarnation, Jesus was a perfect human, and He died as a mere human. When He died, it was not upon a cross but on an upright stake. *Awake!* magazine (a Watchtower publication) states that "no biblical evidence even intimates that Jesus died on a cross."[2] The cross is viewed as a pagan religious symbol that the Christian church adopted in its early years due to Satan's influence.

Three days later Jesus was resurrected—not physically, but as an invisible spirit creature. In Watchtower theology, Jesus's human body could not have been resurrected, for it was given as a permanent ransom sacrifice. "Having given up his flesh for the life of the world, Christ could never take it again and become a man once more."[3] Though now an invisible spirit creature, Jesus nevertheless proved the reality of His resurrection to His followers by appearing to them in fleshly bodies, much like angels appeared to human beings throughout biblical history. "Like those angels, he had the power to construct and to disintegrate those fleshly bodies at will, for the purpose of proving visibly that he had been resurrected."[4]

Since the Watchtower teaches that Jesus was resurrected from the dead as an invisible spirit creature, it also teaches that the second coming would be invisible. This event allegedly occurred in 1914. Since that time, Christ has reportedly been reigning as king of the earth through the Watchtower Society.

Falsehoods to Watch For

- There are two gods. Jesus is a mighty god. The Father is God Almighty.
- Multiple Bible verses are cited to support the idea that Jesus is inferior to the Father.

Important Points to Introduce

- There is only one God, and He is triune.
- Jesus is not a lesser god than God the Father.
- Jesus was and is Yahweh.

Eavesdropping on a Conversation

Notice how I transition in this conversation from a topic of lesser importance to a topic of greater importance—in this case, debunking the Watchtower view that Jesus is a lesser god.

JEHOVAH'S WITNESS: Good morning. We're representatives of the Watchtower Society. Do you have a few minutes?

CHRISTIAN: Okay. You're Jehovah's Witnesses, right? [Silently pray the open-the-heart prayer.]

JEHOVAH'S WITNESS: Yes. And one of the things I appreciate about being a Jehovah's Witness is the great unity that exists among us. This is in contrast to the disunity and division that is typical among various Christian denominations. We have a unity that no other Christian group has.

CHRISTIAN: That's an interesting claim. What led you to that conclusion?

JEHOVAH'S WITNESS: Well, Christian denominations have different views on different doctrines, and they also disagree on rituals in the church. Jehovah's Witnesses are not like that. We enjoy a perfect unity.

CHRISTIAN: Well, I know that there are some other groups that claim perfect unity. For example, the Mormons often claim perfect unity. Members of the Unification church have also often claimed perfect unity. Would you say that the Mormons and the Unification church are in the truth because they claim perfect unity?

JEHOVAH'S WITNESS: No. I doubt they have unity like the Jehovah's Witnesses do. And there are other problems in these groups.

CHRISTIAN: It seems to me that the idea of unity among members is not really a good gauge of what is and what isn't true. For example, members of the Masonic Lodge have impressive unity, but I certainly don't agree with their idea that all the religions of the world are pointing to the same God using different names, do you?

JEHOVAH'S WITNESS: No, I don't.

CHRISTIAN: It also seems to me that the New Testament church experienced some disunity. For example, Paul had to talk to the Corinthian Christians about their disunity, as we see in the first chapter of 1 Corinthians. But he never said they weren't true Christians just because they had disunity. In fact, he indicated throughout the rest of the book that they were true Christians despite their disunity. What's your take on that?

JEHOVAH'S WITNESS: Okay. Fair enough. That's an interesting observation.

CHRISTIAN: [Smile.] Our discussion makes me wonder about something. As a Jehovah's Witness, you're led by the Watchtower Society, right?

JEHOVAH'S WITNESS: That is correct.

CHRISTIAN: Are you free, as a Jehovah's Witness, to question the Watchtower Society or to not go along with a particular teaching of the Watchtower Society?

JEHOVAH'S WITNESS: Well, we believe that the Watchtower Society is the mouthpiece of Jehovah on earth. So we do not question the Society.

CHRISTIAN: That's what I thought. So if no Jehovah's Witness can question the Watchtower Society about one of its teachings, I guess you have no choice but to have perfect unity, right?

JEHOVAH'S WITNESS: That's not really a problem for us.

CHRISTIAN: Really? It kind of sounds like a forced unity to me. Am I wrong in saying that?

JEHOVAH'S WITNESS: Jehovah's Witnesses obey the Watchtower Society as the mouthpiece of Jehovah.

CHRISTIAN: Do you know of any Jehovah's Witnesses personally who have been either disfellowshipped by the Watchtower Society or shunned by other Jehovah's Witnesses for questioning the Watchtower Society?

JEHOVAH'S WITNESS: Well, I've known a few through the years. But a good number of them repented and were brought back into fellowship.

CHRISTIAN: What happened to the others?

JEHOVAH'S WITNESS: They ended up leaving.

CHRISTIAN: [Smile.] Doesn't the fact that there has been some disfellowshipping and shunning undermine the claim of unity?

JEHOVAH'S WITNESS: Compared to many of the Christian denominations, we have much more unity.

CHRISTIAN: Tell me, in terms of religious education, do you read just Watchtower books, or are you also allowed to read Christian books from other Christian publishers?

JEHOVAH'S WITNESS: We read Watchtower books because the Watchtower Society is the mouthpiece of Jehovah on earth.

CHRISTIAN: So you don't read non-Watchtower books?

JEHOVAH'S WITNESS: No.

CHRISTIAN: That's a requirement of the Watchtower Society, right?

JEHOVAH'S WITNESS: Yes.

CHRISTIAN: But you don't think that's forced unity?

JEHOVAH'S WITNESS: We voluntarily submit to the Watchtower Society because we believe it is the mouthpiece of Jehovah on earth.

CHRISTIAN: Are you aware that in the early through mid-1970s, hundreds of thousands of Jehovah's Witnesses left the movement? This rose to a head after 1975 passed, the year the Watchtower Society prophesied that the Old Testament patriarchs—Abraham, Isaac, and Jacob—would be resurrected from the dead and live at a mansion called Beth Sarim in San Diego. If hundreds of thousands of Jehovah's Witnesses left the movement, what does that say about the issue of unity among Jehovah's Witnesses?

JEHOVAH'S WITNESS: I think you may have your facts wrong there.

CHRISTIAN: Really? I'm open to correction if I'm wrong. Would you be willing to consult some *Watchtower* magazines from the early 1970s? I'm glad to provide the documentation for you if you like.[5]

JEHOVAH'S WITNESS: No, that won't be necessary.

CHRISTIAN: I'm not sure if you're aware of this, but the various Christian denominations are in substantial unity on all the essential doctrines of Christianity. They primarily have differences of opinion on nonessential matters—what we might call peripheral issues. Their agreement on the essentials of Christianity comes from their strong commitment to the Bible as the source for truth and their dependence on the Holy Spirit, who guides Christians in the truth. The unity Christians have in these various denominations is not a forced unity.

JEHOVAH'S WITNESS: Well, I don't think they have the kind of unity that exists among Jehovah's Witnesses.

CHRISTIAN: I have another question. As I understand it, when voting on issues, a two-thirds vote is necessary among members of the Governing Body—which is the body that heads up the Watchtower Society. If there were perfect unity among all Jehovah's Witnesses, why is a two-thirds vote necessary? Does this mean there can be disunity even among members of the Governing Body, the top Jehovah's Witnesses in your organization?

JEHOVAH'S WITNESS: Hmm…I haven't thought about that before. I guess that allows for some difference of opinion.

CHRISTIAN: The apostle Paul's teaching on all this seems to be that we are to have unity on the big issues, and if we differ on minor issues, that's okay so long as we do not have a divisive attitude. We see that in 1 Corinthians 1:10. And in Romans 14, Paul even says Christians have the freedom to become convinced in their own minds about these secondary issues.

JEHOVAH'S WITNESS: Okay.

CHRISTIAN: It's kind of like a quilt. A quilt has a basic unity but nevertheless has a variety of different patches on it. Certainly Paul never taught that Christians are to attain unity by submitting to an organization or agency through which doctrinal teaching is authoritatively disseminated and enforced.

JEHOVAH'S WITNESS: I've never heard it put that way before. I'll have to give that some thought.

CHRISTIAN: Good. I hope you do. A moment ago I mentioned how Christian denominations have substantial unity on the essential doctrines of Christianity. One of the biggies is the absolute deity of Jesus Christ. Can I ask you about your view of Jesus's identity as God?

JEHOVAH'S WITNESS: Sure. We believe that the heavenly Father is God Almighty and that Jesus is a lesser god. Jesus was originally created billions of years ago as the archangel Michael, so he is not God in the same sense as the Father. Many verses of Scripture reveal that Jesus is a lesser god.

CHRISTIAN: Such as…

JEHOVAH'S WITNESS: Well, a foundational verse is John 1:1. In the New World Translation it says that "the Word was a god," and the Word here refers to Jesus. Because there is no definite article "the" in the Greek of this verse, it means Christ is only a god, not God Almighty, like the Father is.

CHRISTIAN: I'm somewhat familiar with this verse. My problem with the Watchtower view relates to what Greek linguists say. They make a very good case for the idea that the Greek word for God without the definite article ("the") doesn't need to be translated as "a god" like the Jehovah's Witnesses do in John 1:1.

JEHOVAH'S WITNESS: The Watchtower makes a good case to the contrary.

CHRISTIAN: To make sure I'm understanding you correctly, you're saying that the Greek word for God without the definite article ("the") always means "a god," whereas the Greek word for God with the definite article means "God," right?

JEHOVAH'S WITNESS: That is correct.

CHRISTIAN: In that case, what do you do with John 20:28, where the Greek word for God with the definite article ("the") is used directly of Jesus Christ? John refers to Jesus, saying, "My Lord and my God." The verse reads literally from the Greek: "The Lord of me and the God of me." Clearly in this verse, Jesus is the God and not just a god.

JEHOVAH'S WITNESS: Well, we believe John was just expressing surprise at seeing Jesus resurrected. He was communicating something like, "My God! You're alive!" He wasn't really saying Jesus was actually God.

CHRISTIAN: [Smile.] But that's not what the text says. Thomas says to Jesus, "My Lord and My God," and he does so in a worshipful context. Besides, if Thomas was saying "My God!" in the way you suggested, that would be using God's name in vain, and Jesus surely would have corrected him. The truth is, there are a number of verses in the New Testament where the Greek word for God with the definite article refers to Jesus, including in the Gospel of John. As well, Greek scholars around the world almost all say that the word "God" used of Jesus in John 1:1 does not mean "a god" but rather "God."

JEHOVAH'S WITNESS: We can't go along with that because Scripture is elsewhere clear that Jesus was a created being. In Colossians 1:15 Jesus is called the firstborn of all creation, meaning that he came into being at a point in time and therefore isn't eternal deity.

CHRISTIAN: Well, that's a great verse, and I'm glad you brought it up. Are you open to hearing my take on that verse?

JEHOVAH'S WITNESS: Well, okay.

CHRISTIAN: The word "firstborn" in the Bible often carries the meaning of "first in rank, preeminent one, heir." This is illustrated in the person of David. He was the youngest of Jesse's sons, but he is called the firstborn in Psalm 89:27 because he became first in rank as Israel's king. Likewise, even though Ephraim was not actually the first son born to Joseph, he was nevertheless called the firstborn in Jeremiah 31:9 because of his preeminent position. In similar fashion, Jesus is called the firstborn of creation, not because He was the first to come into being in the creation, but rather because He is first in rank and preeminent over creation.

JEHOVAH'S WITNESS: I'm not sure that makes good sense.

CHRISTIAN: [Smile.] Well, consider the context of Colossians 1. Jesus is called the firstborn in verse 15. Then, in the very next verse, we are told that Christ Himself created the creation. Doesn't it make sense that He who created the creation is first in rank and preeminent over it?

JEHOVAH'S WITNESS: Well, I've never heard it put that way before. I'll have to think about it. But this preeminent interpretation does not seem to gel with other verses, like John 14:28, where Jesus Himself acknowledges that the Father is greater than he is.

CHRISTIAN: How do you understand Jesus's words, "My Father is greater than I"?

JEHOVAH'S WITNESS: We take it to mean that the Father is God Almighty, and Jesus is a lesser god.

CHRISTIAN: Actually, I think this verse makes perfect sense interpreting Jesus as absolute deity, just like the Father.

JEHOVAH'S WITNESS: How so?

CHRISTIAN: Well, when Jesus spoke these words, the Father was up in heaven, in a perfectly holy environment, with angels singing praises to His name. Meanwhile, Jesus was in a state of great humiliation on earth, being persecuted by Jewish religious leaders and about to be crucified like a criminal. Jesus was thus speaking *positionally* in John 14:28. He was essentially saying, "My Father, who is exalted in heaven, is positionally greater than I, as I am suffering, persecuted, and about to be executed down here on earth."

JEHOVAH'S WITNESS: But what about 1 Corinthians 11:3? This verse tells us that "the head of Christ is God." This fits with Jesus's statement in John 14:28 that the Father is greater than Christ.

CHRISTIAN: Well, I can understand why you'd say that. But I want you to notice something. First Corinthians 11:3 also says that the husband is the head of the wife. So let me ask you a question. Do the husband and wife have the same natures as human beings?

JEHOVAH'S WITNESS: Obviously.

CHRISTIAN: That's what Genesis 1:26-28 teaches, right? Both the man and woman were created as human beings, and both were created in the image of God.

JEHOVAH'S WITNESS: Okay.

CHRISTIAN: So, back to 1 Corinthians 11:3. Even though the husband and wife have the same human nature, the husband is nevertheless the head over the wife, right?

JEHOVAH'S WITNESS: Okay. So…?

CHRISTIAN: Well, the point I'm driving at is that even though the Father and the Son have the same divine nature, the Father is nevertheless in authority over Jesus the Son. Put another way, just because the Father is the head of Christ, that doesn't mean that Christ has a lesser divine nature than the Father.

JEHOVAH'S WITNESS: Okay, I think I understand your position. But you yourself just acknowledged that Jesus is God's son. The very title of son indicates that he is lesser than the Father.

CHRISTIAN: Does it really? How so?

JEHOVAH'S WITNESS: The fact that Jesus is the son indicates he is a lesser being than the Father, and taken with the other verses I've mentioned, indicates that he is a lesser deity than the Father. If Jesus were God Almighty, he would be called "the Father."

CHRISTIAN: [Smile.] Okay, I think I see your point. But let's explore what Scripture actually teaches. It is true that the New Testament calls Jesus the Son of God. John 3:16 is a good example. But when Jesus claimed to be the Son of God, the Jewish leaders understood Jesus to be saying that He had the same divine nature as the Father. For example, in John 5:18 we read "The Jews were seeking all the more to kill him, because not only was he breaking the Sabbath, but he was even calling God his own Father, making himself equal with God." So in Jesus's claim of sonship, He was essentially saying, "I have the same nature as my Father."

JEHOVAH'S WITNESS: Well, I'm not sure about that.

CHRISTIAN: Okay, let me put it this way. Do you have any children?

JEHOVAH'S WITNESS: I have a son.

CHRISTIAN: Okay. Does your son have the same human nature that you do? Obviously so, right?

JEHOVAH'S WITNESS: Okay.

CHRISTIAN: Likewise, the fact that Jesus is the Son of God indicates that He has the same divine nature as the Father. Do you mind if I give you a little linguistic background?

JEHOVAH'S WITNESS: Okay.

CHRISTIAN: Among the ancients, the phrase "son of" was sometimes taken to mean "same nature as." The phrase is often used this way in the Old Testament. For example, the phrase "sons of the prophets" meant "prophets" (1 Kings 20:35). "Sons of the singers" meant "singers" (Nehemiah 12:28). Likewise, "Son of God" among the ancient Jews meant "God" and represented a claim to undiminished deity. This is why, when Jesus claimed to be the Son of God, the Jewish leaders replied, "We have a law, and according to that law he ought to die because he has made himself the Son of God." That's John 19:7. It seems clear that Jesus's claim to be the Son of God amounts to saying "I am God, just as the Father is." That's the way the Jewish leaders understood Him.

JEHOVAH'S WITNESS: Okay. I've never heard that before.

CHRISTIAN: I guess the thing I'm trying to drive home to you is that there is massive evidence in the Bible that Jesus truly is God. For example, Isaiah 43:11 says that only God is the Savior. But Titus 2:13-14 tells us that Jesus is our great God and Savior. Isaiah 44:24 tells us that only God is the Creator, but John 1:3 says that Jesus is the Creator. In Isaiah 6:1-5, we are told that the prophet Isaiah beheld Jehovah's glory, but in John 12:41 we are told that Isaiah actually beheld Jesus's glory.

JEHOVAH'S WITNESS: I think the Watchtower has a different take on all those verses, so I'd have to check them out later.

CHRISTIAN: In view of the things I've told you previously, you might want to give serious consideration about whether you want to trust the Watchtower Society and whether it has been telling you the truth. I strongly urge you to read the Bible alone, using a good translation, such as the English Standard Version, the New American Standard Bible, the New International Version, or the New Living Translation. I can tell you that the Bible has been my one and only source about God and Jesus, and the Jesus of the Bible—who Himself is absolute deity—has set me free from my sins. I have a close personal relationship with Him, and I know beyond any shadow of a doubt that if I were to die today, I'd go straight to heaven, where I'll be with Him for all eternity. You, too, can have that assurance. Jesus can set you free too. You can have an intimate relationship with Him. May I explain how? [If he or she responds affirmatively, share the gospel, including plenty of joyful personal testimony. See chapter 19, "Conversations About Salvation."]

Conversation Highlights

Allow me to highlight a few tactical points from this conversation.

- I debunked the claim that the Jehovah's Witnesses' unity proves that they are God's true people. Because the unity claim is one of their most common selling points, I spent a bit more time on it.

- I patiently but persistently corrected misinterpretations of verses about Jesus.

- I not only corrected errors about Jesus but also presented a positive case for Jesus's absolute deity.

- I closed by giving a brief testimony of what Jesus has done in my life. Whenever you feel it's appropriate, you can give a brief testimony that relates to the topic of your discussion. If you've been talking about Jesus, give a brief testimony about what Jesus has done for you. If you've been talking about grace, give a brief testimony on how appreciative you are for the gospel of grace, for you could never earn your salvation. Your testimony is something the Jehovah's Witness will always remember.

Digging Deeper

You may be interested in more in-depth information on the Jehovah's Witnesses' view of Jesus's alleged inferiority and the specific Bible verses they cite to support it. If so, I invite you to consult my book *Reasoning from the Scriptures with the Jehovah's Witnesses* (2009 edition), pages 121–172.

13

Conversations About Jesus's Crucifixion

———⟨∞⟩———

Jehovah's Witnesses do not believe Jesus was crucified on a cross. "The evidence indicates that Jesus did not die on the traditional cross."[1] Indeed, "no biblical evidence even intimates that Jesus died on a cross."[2] Rather, they claim, "Jesus most likely was executed on an upright stake without any crossbeam."[3]

In support of this idea, Jehovah's Witnesses claim that one of the meanings of the Greek word translated "cross" (*stauros*) is "upright stake." The Watchtower book *Reasoning from the Scriptures* tells us, "In classical Greek, this word meant merely an upright stake, or pale."[4] They cite *The Imperial Bible-Dictionary*, which claims, "The Greek word for cross [*stauros*] properly signified a stake, an upright pole, or piece of paling, on which anything might be hung...Even amongst the Romans the *crux* (from which our cross is derived) appears to have been originally an upright pole."[5]

Jehovah's Witnesses claim that the cross is an ancient pagan religious symbol. In pre-Christian times, it was allegedly a symbol connected with some form of nature worship. This symbol was reportedly adopted by the church in its early years under the influence of Satan. The church therefore became paganized in its early years, and those pagan influences continue to the present day.

For this reason, the Watchtower claims that Christians who wear crucifixes commit idolatry. They claim that inanimate objects "if venerated may lead to breaking God's commandments. Among the most prominent is the cross. For centuries it has been used by people in Christendom as part of their worship. Soon God will execute his judgments against all false religions. Those who cling to them will suffer their fate."[6]

Falsehoods to Watch For

- Jesus was executed not on a cross but on an upright stake.
- The cross was an ancient pagan symbol.
- This pagan symbol infiltrated the early Christian church.
- The church thus became paganized.
- It is idolatrous to wear a crucifix.

Important Points to Introduce

- Jesus was indeed crucified on a cross, not on an upright stake.
- The church adopted the symbol not from pagans but from the instrument of Jesus's death on our behalf.
- Christians often wear a crucifix not because they venerate or worship it, but because it represents the Savior, Jesus, whom they worship.
- No idolatry is involved.

Eavesdropping on a Conversation

Notice how I transition in this conversation from a topic of little importance to a topic of greater importance—in this case, Jesus's crucifixion on a cross.

JEHOVAH'S WITNESS: Good afternoon. My colleague and I are visiting your neighborhood this afternoon. We are Jehovah's Witnesses and attend the Kingdom Hall not too far from here. Do you have a minute to chat?

CHRISTIAN: Okay. [Silently pray the open-the-heart prayer.]

JEHOVAH'S WITNESS: As you probably know, Jesus often preached about the kingdom during his short ministry. One thing Jehovah's Witnesses are well known for is preaching about the kingdom.

Have you noticed how many Christian denominations today largely ignore preaching about God's kingdom?

CHRISTIAN: Well, I've not thought much about it. Is it your view that one test of being God's true people is the preaching of the kingdom?

JEHOVAH'S WITNESS: Well, it's not the only indication of being God's true people, but it is certainly a key indicator.

CHRISTIAN: Are you aware that the Mormons also teach a lot about the kingdom? Would you say they are God's true people?

JEHOVAH'S WITNESS: Ah…no, we wouldn't.

CHRISTIAN: What about Bible-believing Christians, such as myself. I know I've heard sermons in my church on God's kingdom. [Smile.] Does that mean I am part of the true people of God?

JEHOVAH'S WITNESS: Okay, I see where you're going.

CHRISTIAN: [Smile.] My point is that just because Jehovah's Witnesses preach about the kingdom doesn't in itself indicate they are God's true people. Am I fair to say that?

JEHOVAH'S WITNESS: I see your point. I wouldn't disagree with that.

CHRISTIAN: I'm glad to hear it. I think the real issue is whether or not the group believes in and teaches the truth as revealed in the Bible. Take Jesus's death on the cross as an example. That doctrine is certainly at the heart of the New Testament. What is your view of Jesus's death on the cross?

JEHOVAH'S WITNESS: Well, we don't believe that Jesus was crucified on a cross. We believe he was crucified on an upright stake.

CHRISTIAN: What brought you to that conclusion?

JEHOVAH'S WITNESS: The cross is actually an ancient pagan religious symbol. At some point in early church history, Satan seized control of ecclesiastical authorities and through them introduced this pagan symbol into the church.

CHRISTIAN: So, what about Christians who wear crucifixes? Are they actually pagans without knowing it?

JEHOVAH'S WITNESS: We believe that because the cross is a pagan religious symbol, wearing crucifixes constitutes a form of idolatry.

CHRISTIAN: [Smile.] On what basis do you say that Jesus was crucified on an upright stake?

JEHOVAH'S WITNESS: The Greek word translated "cross" in many modern Bible translations actually means "upright stake" or "pale." Since we want to be faithful to the original languages, it seems clear that Jesus was crucified not on a cross but on an upright stake.

CHRISTIAN: Well, I've actually done a bit of study on this. I'd like to share a few things in response, if you don't mind. Is that okay with you?

JEHOVAH'S WITNESS: Sure.

CHRISTIAN: First, did you know that early Watchtower literature, such as *Watchtower* magazines from the late 1920s, actually taught that Jesus died on a cross and not on an upright stake? Some of the early *Watchtower* magazines even featured sketches of Jesus on a cross. This was also taught in the early Watchtower book *Reconciliation*, published in the late 1920s. Are you aware of this?

JEHOVAH'S WITNESS: No, but I'm not sure you've got your facts straight. This is the first I've heard of it.

CHRISTIAN: I think it would be worth your while to check it out. After all, if the cross is a pagan symbol, this would mean that the Watchtower Society was engulfed in paganism, right?

JEHOVAH'S WITNESS: I'll have to check that out.

CHRISTIAN: Actually, the Watchtower Society admits it. *The 1975 Yearbook of Jehovah's Witnesses* conceded that beginning with a 1931 issue of *The Watchtower* magazine, the cross was no longer featured on the cover of *Watchtower* magazines. Then, in the 1970s and 1980s, the Watchtower featured articles claiming that there was no biblical evidence that Jesus died on a cross, but rather died on an upright stake. So again, if the cross is a pagan symbol, this means the Watchtower Society was once engulfed in paganism.

JEHOVAH'S WITNESS: Okay, well, I'll have to look into that further.

CHRISTIAN: I can help provide you with detailed documentation, if you like.[7]

JEHOVAH'S WITNESS: Okay, but no thanks.

CHRISTIAN: Don't get me wrong. I don't think the cross is a symbol of paganism. All I'm saying is that it's a bit strange for today's Watchtower Society to condemn other Christian groups for what it once practiced. Does that make sense?

JEHOVAH'S WITNESS: I understand your point.

CHRISTIAN: Great! I've also done a bit of study on the Greek word translated "cross" in the New Testament. I discovered that the word can refer to an instrument of execution in a variety of different shapes.

JEHOVAH'S WITNESS: What do you mean?

CHRISTIAN: Well, it can refer to a wooden structure shaped like a capital T, or shaped like a capital X, or shaped like a plus sign, or, less frequently, shaped as an upright stake with no crossbeam. The word can refer to an upright stake, but it is actually used more frequently for one of these other shapes.

JEHOVAH'S WITNESS: I've not heard that before.

CHRISTIAN: You obtained the teaching about the upright stake from Watchtower literature, right?

JEHOVAH'S WITNESS: Yes.

CHRISTIAN: I know that the Watchtower Society is supposed to be Jehovah's mouthpiece on earth, but if what I've told you is correct, and the Watchtower Society flipped positions on Jesus being crucified on a cross, what would that say about the Watchtower Society as the mouthpiece of God?

JEHOVAH'S WITNESS: Hmm…I don't think the Watchtower Society is wrong.

CHRISTIAN: But you will check out the facts I've shared with you, right?

JEHOVAH'S WITNESS: I guess I will.

CHRISTIAN: I'd like to read you a quote from the New World Translation. It's from John 20:25, and the verse refers to the person known
as doubting Thomas. "Consequently the other disciples would say
to him: 'We have seen the Lord!' But he said to them: 'Unless I
see in his hands the print of the nails and stick my finger into the
print of the nails and stick my hand into his side, I will certainly
not believe.'" Have you ever thought about the implication of the
plural word "nails" as related to the theory of the upright stake?

JEHOVAH'S WITNESS: What do you mean?

CHRISTIAN: If Jesus were crucified on an upright stake, only one
nail through His hands would be necessary. But nails were used,
evidently one for each hand on different sides of the crossbeam.

JEHOVAH'S WITNESS: Well, it's possible several nails could be used on
his hands on an upright stake.

CHRISTIAN: Can I read you another Bible passage?

JEHOVAH'S WITNESS: Okay.

CHRISTIAN: It's John 21:18-19. In this passage, Jesus spoke to Peter
about Peter's own eventual crucifixion. Jesus said to him, "'Truly,
truly, I say to you, when you were young, you used to dress yourself, and walk wherever you wanted; but when you are old, you will
stretch out your hands, and another will dress you, and carry you
where you do not want to go.' (This he said to show by what kind
of death he was to glorify God.)" In other words, Peter would be
crucified, and in the process, his hands would be stretched out, as
on a crossbeam.

JEHOVAH'S WITNESS: Okay, well, that's talking about Peter, not about
Jesus.

CHRISTIAN: True. But by such words Jesus was telling us something
about crucifixions. He was telling us that in crucifixions, one's
arms are outstretched on the crossbeam, which would be impossible on an upright stake.

JEHOVAH'S WITNESS: Okay, well, maybe.

CHRISTIAN: Would I be pushing things too far to share yet another
verse? I'll be brief. Is that okay?

JEHOVAH'S WITNESS: Okay.

CHRISTIAN: Matthew 27:37 tells us, "Over his head they put the charge against him, which read, 'This is Jesus, the King of the Jews.'" So here's the question. If Jesus was crucified on an upright stake, wouldn't the sign be nailed above his hands and not His head?

JEHOVAH'S WITNESS: Well, I guess that's a good point. I'm not sure how to answer.

CHRISTIAN: That's okay. But in view of all of these facts I've shared with you, I think you can see why I don't think the cross is a symbol of paganism. Rather, it is a symbol of Christ's death on our behalf. This being so, I don't think wearing a crucifix is idolatrous.

JEHOVAH'S WITNESS: Scripture's got some pretty stern warnings against idolatry.

CHRISTIAN: I believe you are right. Can you tell me the Scriptures you have in mind?

JEHOVAH'S WITNESS: Well, the New World Translation renders 1 Corinthians 10:14, "Therefore, my beloved ones, flee from idolatry." All forms of idolatry are condemned by Jehovah.

CHRISTIAN: [Smile.] I agree completely that we are to flee from all forms of idolatry. The problem is, nothing in this verse even remotely relates to the issue of wearing a crucifix. Christians do not venerate the cross itself. Rather, they worship the person who died on it. The cross is full of meaning to Christians only because it represents Christ's death on our behalf.

JEHOVAH'S WITNESS: Well, what about Exodus 20:4-5? The New World Translation renders this passage, "You must not make for yourself a carved image or a form like anything that is in the heavens above or that is on the earth underneath or that is in the waters under the earth. You must not bow down to them nor be induced to serve them, because I Jehovah your God am a God exacting exclusive devotion, bringing punishment for the error of fathers upon sons, upon the third generation and upon the fourth generation, in the case of those who hate me."

CHRISTIAN: Well, that's certainly a powerful passage. But again, I see no connection to the issue of wearing a crucifix. The backdrop of this passage is that the Egyptians—who had recently enslaved the Israelites—made idols and images of false gods that resembled things in heaven (angelic beings), on the earth (humans and animals), and in the sea (sea creatures). The true God said that such images should not be made. One must be faithful to the true God alone. No competing deities will be tolerated. Does that make sense?

JEHOVAH'S WITNESS: Well, perhaps. But the wearing of a crucifix may violate the spirit of the passage.

CHRISTIAN: Keep in mind that Christians do not bow down before and worship crosses. Rather, they exalt Christ alone—and for that reason some Christians wear a crucifix, which points to their worshipful attitude toward Him. Personally, I am profoundly thankful for the message of the cross. You see, I can't save myself. I'm too sinful. I could never be good enough to be saved. But when Jesus died on the cross, He took my sins upon Him. He took my place. He took what was mine (my sin) so that He could give me what was His (eternal salvation). So when I think of the cross, I am full of praise and worship to Him for what He has done.

My friend, you can't be saved by being obedient to the man-made Watchtower Society. You can only be saved by trusting in the Savior, who died on the cross. Can we spend a few minutes talking about the truth that can set you free? [If the Jehovah's Witness answers yes, share the gospel, including lots of joyful personal testimony. See chapter 19, "Conversations About Salvation."]

Conversation Highlights

Allow me to highlight a few tactical points from this conversation.

- I challenged the trustworthiness of the Watchtower Society—allegedly Jehovah's mouthpiece—by showing how it flipped positions on the issue of the cross. As we have seen, my basic strategy in every meeting is twofold: to dialogue (and bring correction) on at least one major doctrine, and also to challenge the trustworthiness of the Watchtower Society.

- I sought not only to correct their view of the cross as an instrument of death but also to point to the incredible significance of Christ's death on that cross.

- I offered to provide documentation on some of the assertions I made. This in itself adds credibility to the assertions, for no one offers documentation if it does not exist.

- Yet again I gave some personal testimony, knowing that this will impact the Jehovah's Witness more than a mere sharing of doctrinal facts. I was also poised to share the gospel at the end of the conversation.

Digging Deeper

You may be interested in more in-depth information on the Jehovah's Witnesses' view of the cross and the specific Bible verses they cite to support it. If so, I invite you to consult my book *Reasoning from the Scriptures with the Jehovah's Witnesses* (2009 edition), pages 397–403.

14

Conversations About Jesus's Resurrection

———∞∞∞———

Jehovah's Witnesses believe Jesus was resurrected not physically but spiritually. The Watchtower book *Studies in the Scriptures* asserts, "We deny that He was raised in the flesh, and challenge any statement to that effect as being unscriptural."[1] *Let Your Name Be Sanctified*, another Watchtower book, tells us that "Jesus was raised to life as an invisible spirit. He did not take up again that body in which he had been killed as a human sacrifice to God."[2] Jesus was allegedly resurrected as the archangel Michael.

Though Jehovah's Witnesses say Jesus is now an invisible spirit creature, they also say Jesus proved the reality of His resurrection to His followers by appearing to them in fleshly bodies, much as angels have appeared to human beings throughout biblical history. "Like those angels, he had the power to construct and to disintegrate those fleshly bodies at will, for the purpose of proving visibly that he had been resurrected."[3] We are told that "in order to convince Thomas of who he was, he used a body with wound holes."[4]

As to what happened to Jesus's human body following His spiritual resurrection, we are told that it "was disposed of by Jehovah God, dissolved into its constituent elements or atoms."[5] Indeed, it "was disposed of by God's power."[6]

At the time of His ascension into heaven, Jesus allegedly dissolved whatever materialized body He was in at the moment and assumed spiritual form. "While Jesus began his ascent in a physical form, thus making possible his being seeable by his watching disciples, there is no basis for assuming that he continued to retain a material form after the cloud interposed itself."[7] Indeed, "while they are still looking on, Jesus begins rising heavenward, and then a cloud obscures him from their sight. After dematerializing his fleshly body, he ascends to heaven as a spirit person."[8]

Falsehoods to Watch For

- Jesus was resurrected not physically but spiritually.
- Jesus was resurrected as the archangel Michael.
- Jehovah disposed of Jesus's human body.
- Jesus materialized various bodies to prove His resurrection.
- At His ascension, Jesus permanently dematerialized after passing through the clouds.

Important Points to Introduce

- Jesus was resurrected physically in the same body that was put to death on the cross.
- Jesus was resurrected as a human, not as an angel or spirit.
- Jehovah's Witnesses misinterpret the Scripture verses they cite in favor of their view.

Eavesdropping on a Conversation

Notice how I transition in this conversation from a topic of little importance to a topic of greater importance—in this case, the physical resurrection of Jesus Christ.

JEHOVAH'S WITNESS: Good morning. You have a beautiful neighborhood. We're Jehovah's Witnesses, and we're visiting your area today. Can we chat for a few minutes?

CHRISTIAN: Sure. [Silently pray the open-the-heart prayer.]

JEHOVAH'S WITNESS: Why do you think so many Christian denominations do not base all their beliefs on the Bible alone?

CHRISTIAN: Well, I'm aware that certain denominations, such as

Roman Catholic and Eastern Orthodox churches, utilize tradition in their beliefs.

JEHOVAH'S WITNESS: What about Protestant churches? Do you think that all Protestant beliefs are based on the Bible alone?

CHRISTIAN: I'm a member of a Protestant church myself, and we base our doctrines on the Bible.

JEHOVAH'S WITNESS: Does your church give any credence to the creeds, such as the Apostles' Creed?

CHRISTIAN: We do believe the creeds contain doctrinal truth, but only insofar as they accurately reflect Scripture. The ultimate source of our beliefs is Scripture, which alone is inspired by God. Is it your view that the use of creeds is wrong?

JEHOVAH'S WITNESS: Well, creeds are man-made documents. The Jehovah's Witnesses use the Bible alone for all their beliefs. We therefore do not subscribe to any man-made doctrines the way so many Protestant and Catholic denominations do.

CHRISTIAN: I find it interesting that you say that.

JEHOVAH'S WITNESS: Why so?

CHRISTIAN: Do the Jehovah's Witnesses really use just the Bible alone? Don't you have to utilize Watchtower publications to tell you what Scripture means? Doesn't the Watchtower Society teach that without its vast literature, people have no hope of understanding the Bible?

JEHOVAH'S WITNESS: The Watchtower Society is Jehovah's mouthpiece on earth. God directs his people through this Society.

CHRISTIAN: [Smile.] I understand that you believe that. But I want to clarify your view. Since *not* using Watchtower literature is not an option for Jehovah's Witnesses, is it true to say that Jehovah's Witnesses use the Bible alone?

JEHOVAH'S WITNESS: Okay, I see your point. But everything the Watchtower Society teaches is correct because it is Jehovah's organization, and He guides every aspect of it.

CHRISTIAN: I understand that you believe that. But I think there's

pretty good evidence that the Watchtower Society is not teaching
God's truth. No offense intended.

JEHOVAH'S WITNESS: None taken. But what do you mean?

CHRISTIAN: Well, one important factor relates to the number of doctrinal changes the Watchtower Society has made through the years.
At one time the Watchtower taught that Jesus died on a cross, but
now it says He died on an upright stake. At one time the Watchtower taught that Jesus should be worshipped, but now it says
Jesus should merely be shown obeisance. At one time the Watchtower taught that people should not receive vaccinations, but now
it says that vaccinations are okay. The Society changed its mind a
number of times regarding when the end of the world would take
place—including 1914, 1925, the early 1940s, and 1975. So here is
my question: If the Watchtower Society is really guided by Jehovah, why does the Watchtower Society keep changing its mind?
Does this mean Jehovah changed His mind, or does the Watchtower Society keep getting it wrong?

JEHOVAH'S WITNESS: Wow. I'm not sure the things you just said are
correct.

CHRISTIAN: Would you consider looking into it? Why don't you do a
little research. The next time you come by, let me know what you
discover. If I end up being wrong on anything, I promise to give
thoughtful consideration to any evidence you bring me. By the
way, I'm happy to provide you with some documentation from
Watchtower sources if you like.[9]

JEHOVAH'S WITNESS: Well, no thanks.

CHRISTIAN: Okay. The offer stands. So let me know if you change
your mind.

JEHOVAH'S WITNESS: Okay.

CHRISTIAN: Now that I think about it, it's not just the changes that
bother me about the Watchtower Society. It's also some of its cur-
rent teachings.

JEHOVAH'S WITNESS: What do you mean?

CHRISTIAN: Let's take a key biblical doctrine as an example—the resurrection of Jesus Christ. Do you believe that Jesus was physically resurrected from the dead?

JEHOVAH'S WITNESS: No, we believe that Jesus was spiritually resurrected from the dead. Jesus was raised with a spirit body.

CHRISTIAN: Can I ask you what led you to that conclusion?

JEHOVAH'S WITNESS: Well, Scripture seems rather clear on it. First Peter 3:18 in the New World Translation reads, "Why, even Christ died once for all time concerning sins, a righteous [person] for unrighteous ones, that he might lead you to God, he being put to death in the flesh, but being made alive in the spirit."

CHRISTIAN: So you interpret that to mean that Jesus was resurrected in a spirit body?

JEHOVAH'S WITNESS: Yes.

CHRISTIAN: And so you believe it was an invisible resurrection?

JEHOVAH'S WITNESS: Jesus was resurrected as an invisible spirit, yes.

CHRISTIAN: Why didn't He resurrect in His physical body?

JEHOVAH'S WITNESS: Because that is the body he used in his sacrifice for sin. Once given in sacrifice, the body cannot be taken up again in resurrection. He was raised as a spirit because only a spirit body is suitable for life in heaven.

CHRISTIAN: Okay, I think I understand your view. Would you mind if I shared my understanding of all this?

JEHOVAH'S WITNESS: That's fine.

CHRISTIAN: First Peter 3:18 reads, "For Christ also suffered once for sins, the just for the unjust, that He might bring us to God, being put to death in the flesh but made alive by the Spirit" (NKJV). In my understanding, Jesus was not raised *as* a spirit, but was rather raised *by* the spirit—that is, the Holy Spirit.

JEHOVAH'S WITNESS: Are you saying that Jehovah did not raise Jesus from the dead?

CHRISTIAN: [Smile.] Good question. Actually, I think that all three persons of the Trinity were involved in raising Jesus from the dead. Now, I know that as a Jehovah's Witness, you don't believe in the

Trinity, and I'd be glad to chat about that later with you. For now, though, let me say that in addition to 1 Peter 3:18, which teaches that the Holy Spirit raised Jesus from the dead, Scripture also says the Father raised Him from the dead. Acts 2:32 specifically says, "This Jesus God raised up." Not only that, but in John 2:19-21, Jesus said He'd resurrect Himself from the dead. He told the Jewish leaders, "Destroy this temple, and in three days I will raise it up...He was speaking about the temple of his body." Is all this new to you?

JEHOVAH'S WITNESS: Well, I've never heard it explained that way before. But I'm sure the Watchtower has another explanation for all this.

CHRISTIAN: Scripture provides plenty of evidence that Jesus was physically resurrected and not spiritually resurrected. Would you mind if I shared a few thoughts on this?

JEHOVAH'S WITNESS: Okay. But before you do, let's be clear that 1 Corinthians 15:50 says that "flesh and blood cannot inherit God's kingdom." So if Jesus went to heaven, he must have done so in a resurrected spirit body.

CHRISTIAN: That's a good verse, and I'm glad you brought it up. I've done a little study on this. I discovered that the phrase "flesh and blood" was simply a Jewish idiom referring to mortal humanity. Mortal humanity must be made immortal humanity in order to survive in heaven. The perishable must be made imperishable. In the resurrection, we will have immortal, imperishable physical bodies. If I might put it in modern terminology, we'll all need body upgrades in order to live in heaven. Does that make sense?

JEHOVAH'S WITNESS: I'd have to think about it.

CHRISTIAN: Okay. Well, there's something important I want to share with you. When the resurrected Christ appeared to His followers, He said to them, "See my hands and my feet, that it is I myself. Touch me, and see. For a spirit does not have flesh and bones as you see that I have." This is Luke 24:39. Now, notice three things here. First, the resurrected Christ says in this verse that He is not a spirit. Second, His resurrection body is made up of flesh and bones. And third, Christ's physical hands and feet represent physical proof of the materiality of His resurrection from the dead. Does that sound like a spiritual resurrection to you?

JEHOVAH'S WITNESS: Hmm…Doesn't seem to. But we believe that even though Jesus was resurrected with a spirit body, he had the ability to materialize a body to prove to the disciples that he had been resurrected. This was similar to how angels often appeared as men in Bible times.

CHRISTIAN: [Smile.] I understand that the Watchtower teaches that. But when you look at the text, Jesus didn't say that. Jesus's point was that in His resurrection body, He was not a spirit, and He offered hard proof by inviting His followers to touch Him. Remember the verses I cited earlier—John 2:19-21. Jesus said, "Destroy this temple, and in three days I will raise it up." Notice that Jesus says that if the Jews destroy His body by crucifixion, in three days He would raise it up—that is, he'd raise the very same physical body that went into the tomb. So it wasn't a different spirit body that Jesus received at the resurrection; it was the same physical body that died and was buried in the tomb that was raised.

JEHOVAH'S WITNESS: Hmm…Okay. I'll have to think about that.

CHRISTIAN: Notice also that Jesus's resurrection body retained the physical wounds He received at the cross. He revealed these crucifixion scars to the disciples, and He even invited doubting Thomas to physically touch them in John 20:27. Taken at face value, doesn't that verse seem to indicate a permanent, physically resurrected body to you? The idea that Jesus simply materialized a physical body to prove His resurrection seems to reek of misrepresentation on Jesus's part. I find it impossible to believe that Jesus would engage in such duplicitous actions.

JEHOVAH'S WITNESS: I understand your point, but certainly angels made appearances among human beings in biblical times in what appeared to be physical bodies even though they are actually spirits.

CHRISTIAN: The problem is, the angels weren't claiming to be physical beings, as the resurrected Jesus claimed in Luke 24:39. The angels did not deny they were spirits, as Jesus did in Luke 24:39, did they?

JEHOVAH'S WITNESS: Hmm…

CHRISTIAN: Let me share another point. Did you know that the resurrected Christ ate physical food on four different occasions? He did this as a means of proving that He had a real, physical body. We see this in Luke 24:30, 42-43, John 21:12-13, and Acts 1:4 (NIV). Don't you think it would have been deceptive for Jesus to have offered His ability to eat physical food as a proof of His bodily resurrection if He were really only raised as a spirit?

JEHOVAH'S WITNESS: Well, I'm not sure.

CHRISTIAN: Another thing I've discovered in my personal Bible study is that the dead human body is metaphorically compared to a kernel that is sown into the ground, just like planting a seed. That kernel of a dead body blossoms in resurrection. We see this in 1 Corinthians 15:35-44. When you plant a physical seed in the ground, it eventually gives birth to a physical flower. Likewise, when Jesus's dead human body was placed in the tomb, three days later it was physically resurrected.

Now, I have to tell you, I'm sure glad to know that Jesus was physically resurrected from the dead. I say that because Scripture promises that true believers in Jesus Christ will also one day be physically resurrected. We'll all receive body upgrades. There will be no more sickness, no more symptoms, no more pain, and no more death. It will be glorious. But this wondrous destiny is only for those who trust in the true Jesus of the Bible and believe in the one true gospel of grace. How about we spend a little time talking about this gospel of grace? [If the Jehovah's Witness answers affirmatively, share the gospel of grace and include lots of joyful testimony. See chapter 19, "Conversations About Salvation."]

Conversation Highlights

Allow me to highlight a few tactical points from this conversation.

- I continued my two-pronged approach, challenging the trustworthiness of the Watchtower Society and correcting at least one major doctrine.

- I answered objections to the physical resurrection of Christ and presented a positive case for it.

- I offered to provide documentation for some of my assertions. To continue making this point may seem tedious, but Jehovah's Witnesses need to know these assertions can be proved.

- I engineered my closing comments so I was poised to share the gospel of grace and share further personal testimony.

Digging Deeper

You may be interested in more in-depth information on the Jehovah's Witnesses' view of Christ's resurrection and the specific Bible verses they cite to support it. If so, I invite you to consult my book *Reasoning from the Scriptures with the Jehovah's Witnesses* (2009 edition), pages 185–194.

15

Conversations About Jesus's Second Coming

⸎

The Watchtower view of Jesus's resurrection is closely connected to its view of His second coming. Because Jesus was resurrected as an invisible spirit creature, the second coming—or, as the Watchtower puts it, Christ's spiritual presence—is an invisible event as well. This event has allegedly already taken place, and at that time Christ began His reign on earth through the Watchtower Society.

The Watchtower Society claims to be the mouthpiece of Jehovah on earth, yet the Society has changed its position on when this event took place. Early publications of the Watchtower Society claimed the event took place in 1874. We see this especially in *The Studies in the Scriptures* series.[1] In volume four we read, "Our Lord, the appointed King, is now present, since October 1874, A.D."[2] In volume seven we read, "The millennium [during which Christ reigns] began in 1874, with the Return of Christ."[3]

The Watchtower Society now claims that Christ came again invisibly and spiritually in 1914.[4] This essentially means that Christ has been spiritually present since 1914, reigning as King on earth through the Watchtower Society. *The Watchtower* magazine affirms, "The Watchtower has consistently presented evidence to honest-hearted students of Bible prophecy that Jesus's presence in heavenly Kingdom power began in 1914."[5] We are told, "The prophecy of the Bible, fully supported by the physical facts in fulfillment thereof, shows that the second coming of Christ dates from the fall of the year 1914."[6]

Watchtower literature also asserted that the year 1914 would mark the overthrow of human governments and the full establishment of the kingdom of God on earth.[7] This quite obviously did not take place. The Watchtower failed prophecies—as well as their change in dates for the second coming and their multiple changes in doctrine—do not bode well for the Watchtower claim of being the voice of Jehovah on earth.

Falsehoods to Watch For

- The second coming of Christ is an invisible event.
- The second coming—involving Christ's spiritual presence—took place in 1914.
- The second coming essentially involves the beginning of Christ's invisible reign through the Watchtower Society.

Important Points to Introduce

- The second coming of Christ is a physical, visible, and glorious event. Every eye will see Him.
- The second coming is yet future.

Eavesdropping on a Conversation

JEHOVAH'S WITNESS: Good morning. My name is Jay, and my colleague is Tim. We're Jehovah's Witnesses, and we're visiting your area this morning. Do you have a few minutes to talk?

CHRISTIAN: Yes. In fact, I have a question for you. [Smile.] How did you investigate the Jehovah's Witnesses and the Watchtower Society before you decided to join it? Did you consult books written both for and against the Society? [Silently pray the open-the-heart prayer.]

JEHOVAH'S WITNESS: Well, actually, I was going through a tough time in my life. When some Jehovah's Witnesses visited me one Saturday morning, the timing couldn't have been better. Being a part of this organization makes me feel like I'm part of something good. It's also nice to know that I'm in the truth.

CHRISTIAN: I understand. Are you saying that in joining the organization, you did not consult any criticism against the group?

JEHOVAH'S WITNESS: No, I didn't.

CHRISTIAN: [Smile.] I understand. Well, let me ask you this. By the time you joined the Jehovah's Witnesses, had you ever completely read through the Bible?

JEHOVAH'S WITNESS: No. I didn't really start reading the Bible until after I became a Jehovah's Witness.

CHRISTIAN: I see. And these days, most of your reading is in Watchtower literature about the Bible, right?

JEHOVAH'S WITNESS: That's correct.

CHRISTIAN: Do you always look up the individual verses cited in Watchtower publications?

JEHOVAH'S WITNESS: Well, sometimes. Watchtower publications do contain Bible references. That helps me be sure that what I'm reading is biblical.

CHRISTIAN: Were you aware that many groups claim to be Christian and involve many very nice people who cite the Bible a lot and make you feel like you're part of a good group? But some of these groups have either misinterpreted or misrepresented some Bible verses, so they aren't in the truth even though they think they are.

JEHOVAH'S WITNESS: Well, I'm sure that's probably true. But you can trust the Watchtower Society because it is Jehovah's mouthpiece on earth.

CHRISTIAN: Who told you that?

JEHOVAH'S WITNESS: The Watchtower Society.

CHRISTIAN: [Smile.] Gee, that kind of sounds like circular reasoning. Do you know what that is?

JEHOVAH'S WITNESS: I think so, but remind me.

CHRISTIAN: Okay. You're saying that you know that the Watchtower

Society is God's mouthpiece on earth because the Watchtower Society told you so.

JEHOVAH'S WITNESS: Okay, I think I understand your point.

CHRISTIAN: Are you sure you're doing the right thing in supporting this organization? After all, it's got a pretty bad track record.

JEHOVAH'S WITNESS: What do you mean?

CHRISTIAN: Well, contrary to the biblical prophets, the Watchtower Society has given some false prophecies. For example, it predicted that 1914 would mark the overthrow of human governments and the full establishment of God's kingdom on earth. It also predicted that in 1925, Abraham, Isaac, and Jacob would rise from the grave and live in San Diego. Then it predicted that in 1975, human history would end and the thousand-year reign of Christ would begin. Hundreds of thousands of Jehovah's Witnesses left the Watchtower organization after these prophecies failed to pan out. Do you really want to trust your eternal salvation to an organization that first emerged in the nineteenth century and has had such a dismal track record?

JEHOVAH'S WITNESS: Some of the biblical prophets made mistakes, and no one condemned them.

CHRISTIAN: Really? What makes you say that?

JEHOVAH'S WITNESS: Well, Jonah's prediction about the destruction of Nineveh did not come to pass. Jonah as a prophet of God clearly made a mistake.

CHRISTIAN: Actually, Jonah didn't make a mistake. He spoke the exact words God instructed him to speak to the Ninevites. But there was an implied condition in Jonah's exhortation to Nineveh—"Unless you repent, God will destroy you." The fulfillment of the threat of judgment thus depended on the Ninevites' response.

JEHOVAH'S WITNESS: An implied condition? This is the first I've heard of that!

CHRISTIAN: God Himself spoke these words in Jeremiah 18:7-8: "If at any time I declare concerning a nation or a kingdom, that I will pluck up and break down and destroy it, and if that nation, concerning which I have spoken, turns from its evil, I will relent of the disaster that I intended to do to it." Nineveh repented, and God withheld judgment. But Jonah was a true prophet, unlike the Watchtower Society.

JEHOVAH'S WITNESS: Okay, I wasn't aware of that passage. I'll need to give that some further thought.

CHRISTIAN: [Smile.] Good. But while we're on the topic of prophecy, would you mind if we chat a few minutes about the second coming of Jesus Christ?

JEHOVAH'S WITNESS: Sure, that's fine.

CHRISTIAN: Can you tell me what the Watchtower Society teaches about Christ's second coming?

JEHOVAH'S WITNESS: We believe that Christ returned invisibly in 1914 and has been spiritually present with humankind ever since.

CHRISTIAN: Is this idea of an invisible coming related to the Watchtower claim that Jesus was resurrected in a spirit body as the archangel Michael?

JEHOVAH'S WITNESS: Yes. Because Jesus was resurrected in a spirit body, he returned in a spirit body, so he's invisible, like the angels.

CHRISTIAN: On what Bible verse do Jehovah's Witnesses base such an idea?

JEHOVAH'S WITNESS: Well, we think Matthew 24 supports this idea. In fact, in Matthew 24:3, the disciples asked Jesus, "What will be the sign of your presence and of the conclusion of the system of things?" I'm quoting from the New World Translation.

CHRISTIAN: My Bible says, "What will be the sign of your coming and of the close of the age." We believe that verses like this point to an actual physical coming of Christ in the future. But do you think the verse is referring to Christ's spiritual presence since 1914?

JEHOVAH'S WITNESS: Yes. We believe various Scriptures provide us with what we might call a composite sign. This sign involves a number of elements based on several Bible verses, all of which deal with prophecy. For example, today we see nations rising against nations, food shortages, great earthquakes, the outbreak of deadly pestilences, and an increase in lawlessness. Jehovah's true followers are being persecuted, and the good news of the kingdom is being preached around the world. These prophecies make up a composite sign that confirms that we are in the end times and that Christ has been spiritually present since 1914, when all these things started happening. Because world-shattering events have occurred in quick succession since 1914, it is clear that this is the year Christ came and began his spiritual rule.

CHRISTIAN: Wow, that's a lot to take in. Let's back up a bit and deal with one thing at a time. To begin, it seems to me Scripture indicates that the second coming of Christ will not be an invisible event. Rather, every eye will see Him. For example, Jesus Himself promises in Matthew 24:29-30, "Immediately after the tribulation of those days the sun will be darkened, and the moon will not give its light, and the stars will fall from heaven, and the powers of the heavens will be shaken. Then will appear in heaven the sign of the Son of Man, and then all the tribes of the earth will mourn, and they will see the Son of Man coming on the clouds of heaven with power and great glory." Doesn't a plain reading of that text indicate that people will witness the second coming with their own eyes?

JEHOVAH'S WITNESS: Well, we believe that people perceive Christ's presence with their spiritual eyes. They don't physically see him.

CHRISTIAN: Revelation 1:7 says, "Behold, he is coming with the clouds, and every eye will see him, even those who pierced him, and all tribes of the earth will wail on account of him." This verse plainly states that every eye will see him.

JEHOVAH'S WITNESS: Actually, when this verse says that Christ comes with the clouds, it's indicating that he is invisible. After all, when an airplane is in a thick cloud, people on the ground usually cannot see it. People will see Christ, or perceive his presence, with their spiritual eyes.

CHRISTIAN: Why not let the Bible speak for itself? Do you think it's right to superimpose meanings onto the text that are from an organization that didn't even come into being until the late nineteenth century?

JEHOVAH'S WITNESS: Well, the Watchtower speaks for Jehovah.

CHRISTIAN: The text plainly states that every eye will see him. If words mean anything at all, this can't be taken to mean that people spiritually perceive that Christ is present. The Bible states rather plainly that people will physically see him.

JEHOVAH'S WITNESS: What about the clouds?

CHRISTIAN: That's a good question. In Acts 1:9-11, Jesus physically and visibly ascended into heaven. The text tells us that as Christ's followers were watching, Jesus "was lifted up, and a cloud took him out of their sight." Did you know that in Old Testament times, clouds are often associated with the magnificent glory of God? For example, Exodus 16:10 tells us, "As soon as Aaron spoke to the whole congregation of the people of Israel, they looked toward the wilderness, and behold, the glory of the LORD appeared in the cloud." We see this same type of thing in many, many Old Testament verses. In view of this, Acts 1:9-11 indicates that just as Jesus ascended into heaven in a visible great cloud of glory, so the second coming of Christ will involve Christ coming in a visible great cloud of glory. After all, Acts 1:11 quotes God's angels saying to Christ's followers, "This Jesus, who was taken up from you into heaven, will come in the same way as you saw him go into heaven." In other words, just as Jesus ascended visibly and physically in a great cloud of glory, so Christ will come again visibly and physically in a great cloud of glory.

JEHOVAH'S WITNESS: I've never heard it explained that way before.

CHRISTIAN: First Peter 4:13 also refers to Jesus's glory being revealed at the second coming. I did some study on this verse and found out that the word for "revealed" carries the idea of visible disclosure. Christ's glory will be visibly disclosed at His second coming.

JEHOVAH'S WITNESS: Hmm...

CHRISTIAN: Likewise, Titus 2:13 says we are presently awaiting "the appearing of the glory of our great God and Savior Jesus Christ." The word "appearing" in this verse literally means "shining forth." It's going to be awesome.

JEHOVAH'S WITNESS: Okay, but what about Matthew 24:3, where the disciples asked Jesus, "What will be the sign of your presence and of the conclusion of the system of things?" That sounds like Jesus is only spiritually present.

CHRISTIAN: I agree that it sounds that way from the New World Translation. But I've done a lot of study on this issue. From what I've discovered, the Greek word that is rendered "presence" in the New World Translation should actually be translated "coming." In the New Testament, this Greek word typically denotes both a physical arrival and a consequent physical presence. For example, the apostle Paul says in 1 Corinthians 16:17, "I rejoice at the coming of Stephanas and Fortunatus and Achaicus, because they have made up for your absence." Paul says in 2 Corinthians 7:6, "God, who comforts the downcast, comforted us by the coming of Titus." Both these verses use the same Greek word as used of Jesus's second coming. Seen in this way, Matthew 24:3 indicates that Jesus is physically coming again, after which He will remain physically present on earth.

JEHOVAH'S WITNESS: Hmm…Okay. I'll have to look into that further.

CHRISTIAN: Here's something else to think about. Second Timothy 1:10 describes Christ's first coming as "the appearing of our Savior Christ Jesus." The Greek word for appearing here is *epiphaneia*. Interestingly, the second coming of Christ is described as "the appearing of the glory of our great God and Savior Jesus Christ"—using the same Greek word, *epiphaneia*. Just as Christ's first coming was physical and visible, so Christ's second coming will be physical and visible.

JEHOVAH'S WITNESS: So, I guess it goes without saying that you don't think Christ came again back in 1914?

CHRISTIAN: [Smile.] That's true. In my thinking, Matthew 24:29-30 just doesn't square with an invisible coming. It says, "Immediately after the tribulation of those days the sun will be darkened, and the moon will not give its light, and the stars will fall from heaven, and the powers of the heavens will be shaken. Then will appear in heaven the sign of the Son of Man, and then all the tribes of the earth will mourn, and they will see the Son of Man coming on the clouds of heaven with power and great glory." Did any of those things happen in 1914? Did the moon refuse to give its light? Did the stars fall from heaven? Did people around the earth mourn? Did people see Christ coming? The truth is, none of those things happened in 1914. I believe the second coming is yet future, and it will be physical, visible, and glorious.

I'd love to chat with you more about the Bible. Can we set a date right now? And what would you like to talk about the next time you stop by?

Conversation Highlights

- This time around I handled things a bit differently. Instead of waiting for the Jehovah's Witness to launch into his chosen topic of discussion, I asked the first question and steered the conversation from the very start.

- I asked whether the Jehovah's Witness had read the entire Bible before joining the Jehovah's Witnesses.

- I asked whether the Jehovah's Witness had read criticisms against the Watchtower Society before joining.

- I explained the concept of circular reasoning.

- I suggested we set a date for our next meeting. I also tried to clarify the topic so I could be ready for that next meeting.

Digging Deeper

You may be interested in more in-depth information on the Jehovah's Witnesses' view of Christ's second coming and the specific Bible verses they cite to support it. If so, I invite you to consult my book *Reasoning from the Scriptures with the Jehovah's Witnesses* (2009 edition), pages 352–366.

16

Conversations About the Holy Spirit

———— ∞∞∞ ————

Jehovah's Witnesses deny the doctrine of the Trinity (more on this in the next chapter), so the Holy Spirit is obviously not the third person of the Trinity. In fact, Jehovah's Witnesses deny both that the Holy Spirit is a person and that He is God.

The Watchtower Society teaches that the Holy Spirit "is not a person but is a powerful force that God causes to emanate from himself to accomplish his holy will."[1] This force "can be adapted to perform a great variety of operations."[2]

This force plays a critical role in Watchtower theology. For example, this powerful force of God came upon Jesus in the form of a dove at His baptism—a force that enabled Him to perform many miracles (Mark 1:10). Jehovah's Witnesses also claim that "Jehovah's organization alone, in all the earth, is directed by God's holy spirit or active force."[3]

We are told that "Jehovah's active force or spirit is subject to his control and always accomplishes his purpose."[4] Just as electricity can be used by a person to accomplish a variety of tasks, so Jehovah uses the force of the Holy Spirit to accomplish His various tasks.

Falsehoods to Watch For

- The Holy Spirit is not the third person of the Trinity, for the Trinity is a false doctrine.
- The Holy Spirit is not God.
- The Holy Spirit is not a person.
- The Holy Spirit is God's active force in the world, under the control of Jehovah.

Important Points to Introduce

- The Holy Spirit is God.
- The Holy Spirit is a person.
- The Holy Spirit is the third person of the Trinity.
- The Holy Spirit is active in the world, not as a force, but as a person.

Eavesdropping on a Conversation

JEHOVAH'S WITNESS: Good morning. I'm affiliated with the Watchtower Society. Do you have a moment?

CHRISTIAN: Yes. You're a Jehovah's Witness, right? [Silently pray the open-the-heart prayer.]

JEHOVAH'S WITNESS: Yes. You've heard of us?

CHRISTIAN: Yes indeed. Your organization publishes *The Watchtower* magazine, right?

JEHOVAH'S WITNESS: Yes, and I've got a few copies with me today.

CHRISTIAN: You know, I've always wondered something about *The Watchtower* magazine. I notice that both the magazine and Watchtower books often quote from secular encyclopedias, such as *Encyclopedia Britannica,* to support the Watchtower's doctrinal views. The publishers of these encyclopedias are not Jehovah's Witnesses. So why does the Watchtower Society quote from them?

JEHOVAH'S WITNESS: Well, I guess because they've got good scholarship.

CHRISTIAN: But doesn't the Watchtower Society claim to be the mouthpiece of Jehovah?

JEHOVAH'S WITNESS: Yes.

CHRISTIAN: And the truth of Jehovah is disseminated through Watchtower literature, right?

JEHOVAH'S WITNESS: Yes.

CHRISTIAN: So am I to conclude that Jehovah's truth is found in these encyclopedias?

JEHOVAH'S WITNESS: Well, no. I suppose the encyclopedias are cited as scholarly support for the teachings.

CHRISTIAN: [Smile.] The strange thing about all this is that there are articles in these very same encyclopedias that either support or are favorable to evolution, humanism, and naturalism—the idea that there is no supernatural and that nature explains everything. So why would the Watchtower Society want to quote from encyclopedias that teach those kinds of falsehood?

JEHOVAH'S WITNESS: Hmm...the Watchtower never quotes from those articles.

CHRISTIAN: Still, you understand my concern, right? It just seems odd that an organization that claims to be Jehovah's mouthpiece cites secular encyclopedias that have many anti-Jehovah articles.

JEHOVAH'S WITNESS: Okay.

CHRISTIAN: Does the Watchtower Society allow its adherents to read such secular publications to enhance their knowledge of religious things?

JEHOVAH'S WITNESS: No.

CHRISTIAN: So Watchtower leaders are allowed to read them, but average Jehovah's Witnesses aren't allowed to read them?

JEHOVAH'S WITNESS: That is correct.

CHRISTIAN: Are you okay with that?

JEHOVAH'S WITNESS: Well, we are to be obedient to Jehovah's organization.

CHRISTIAN: Is it your opinion that the Watchtower Society, as Jehovah's organization, always quotes these various encyclopedias in context?

JEHOVAH'S WITNESS: Of course.

CHRISTIAN: I've done a little research on this, and I found some problems. For example, the Watchtower Society quoted *Encyclopedia Americana* to the effect that the doctrine of the Trinity is beyond the grasp of human reason. When you look at the article in context, the article actually states that while the doctrine is beyond the grasp of human reason, it is not contrary to reason and may be apprehended by the human mind, even if not fully comprehended by the human mind. Does it sound like the Watchtower Society quoted the article in context to you?

JEHOVAH'S WITNESS: Hmm...I'm not sure about that.

CHRISTIAN: Actually there are many out-of-context quotes in Watchtower literature. I really urge you to look into this thoroughly.

JEHOVAH'S WITNESS: I'll check it out.

CHRISTIAN: Would you like for me to provide you with a list that documents such misquotes?[5] I'm happy to help you.

JEHOVAH'S WITNESS: Well, maybe later.

CHRISTIAN: Okay. You know, contrary to such error, the Bible says that the Holy Spirit is the Spirit of truth and that He guides us in understanding the truth in Scripture. Can we talk about the Holy Spirit for a few minutes?

JEHOVAH'S WITNESS: Okay.

CHRISTIAN: What is your take on the Holy Spirit?

JEHOVAH'S WITNESS: We believe the holy spirit is Jehovah's impersonal active force for accomplishing His will in the world. This powerful force enabled Jesus to perform miracles. Just as the force of electricity can be used to accomplish a great deal, so Jehovah uses the force of the holy spirit to accomplish His purposes.

CHRISTIAN: What made you conclude that the Holy Spirit is an impersonal force and not a person?

JEHOVAH'S WITNESS: For one thing, Scripture speaks of thousands of people being filled by the holy spirit. Such terminology makes sense only if the holy spirit is a force. How would it be possible for thousands of people to be filled with a person?

CHRISTIAN: Well, I think that's a good question. I also think there's a good answer. Ephesians 3:19 speaks of being filled with God Himself. So here's my question. Does the fact that God can fill all things mean that He is not a person?

JEHOVAH'S WITNESS: Hmm...I'm not familiar with that verse. I guess the answer would be no.

CHRISTIAN: Right! Ephesians 4:10 speaks of Christ filling all things. And Ephesians 1:23 speaks of Christ as the one who "fills all in all." Does the fact that Christ can fill all things mean that He is not a person?

JEHOVAH'S WITNESS: Okay, I see where you're going with this.

CHRISTIAN: Good. My point is that both God and Jesus are persons, and they both fill all things, so we can't deny that the Holy Spirit is a person simply because He fills all things.

JEHOVAH'S WITNESS: Okay. I'll have to look into that further. However, a big problem with your view is that if the holy spirit were a person, it would certainly have a name just as the Father and the Son do. The Father's name is Jehovah. The Son's name is Jesus. But the holy spirit does not have a name. So it's not a person like the Father and the Son are.

CHRISTIAN: Personally, I don't see that as a problem. After all, spiritual beings are not always named in Scripture. Rather, they are typically identified by their predominant characteristic. Can I give you an example?

JEHOVAH'S WITNESS: Okay.

CHRISTIAN: Evil spirits are rarely named in Scripture. Rather, they are identified by their particular character. They are identified as being unclean or wicked. Matthew 12:43 and 45 are examples. Likewise, the Holy Spirit is identified by His primary character, which is holiness. So, in my thinking, it's wrong to deny the Holy Spirit's personhood only because He does not have a personal name.

JEHOVAH'S WITNESS: I'm not sure I find that very convincing.

CHRISTIAN: Well, here's something to think about. The Holy Spirit is related to the name of the Father and the Son. In Matthew 28:19 we read, "Go therefore and make disciples of all nations, baptizing them in the name of the Father and of the Son and of the Holy Spirit." Just as the Father and the Son are persons, so the Holy Spirit is a person. All three are identified with the same name.

JEHOVAH'S WITNESS: Well, the use of the word "name" does not always refer to a personal name. For example, the phrase "in the name of the law" has no reference to a person.

CHRISTIAN: I'll grant you that. The problem I see is that in the New Testament, the word "name" is used 228 times, and except for four place names found in the Gospels and the book of Acts, the word always refers to real persons. In Matthew 28:19, it's obvious that since the Father and the Son are persons, the use of the word "name" in association with Father, Son, and Holy Spirit must mean that all three are persons. Does that make sense to you?

JEHOVAH'S WITNESS: I understand what you're saying. But the Watchtower Society tells us that the holy spirit is often personified in Scripture. For example, sin is not a person, but it is sometimes personified in Scripture. In Genesis 4:7 we read, "Sin is crouching at the door. Its desire is for you, but you must rule over it." It makes sin look like a hungry beast ready to attack. Likewise, Scripture sometimes speaks of the holy spirit in personal terms and uses personal pronouns, but these are just personifications.

CHRISTIAN: Have you considered the fact that the Holy Spirit uses personal pronouns of Himself? [Smile.] In Acts 13:2 we read, "While they were worshiping the Lord and fasting, the Holy Spirit said, 'Set apart for me Barnabas and Saul for the work to which I have called them.'" Notice that the Holy Spirit is speaking. Can a personification speak? Notice also that the Holy Spirit uses the personal pronouns "me" and "I" in reference to Himself. Does a personification use personal pronouns of Himself?

JEHOVAH'S WITNESS: I've never thought about that before.

CHRISTIAN: You know, there is a lot of evidence in Scripture that the Holy Spirit is actually a person and not a force. Would you mind if I shared some of the evidence that convinced me personally of this?

JEHOVAH'S WITNESS: Okay.

CHRISTIAN: First of all, the three primary attributes of personality are a mind, emotions, and a will. A force does not have these attributes. If it can be demonstrated that the Holy Spirit has a mind, emotions, and a will, then it becomes clear that He is a person and not a force.

JEHOVAH'S WITNESS: Okay. What verses did you have in mind?

CHRISTIAN: We know the Holy Spirit has a mind because Romans 8:27 tells us the Father "knows what is the mind of the Spirit." We know the Holy Spirit has emotions because Ephesians 4:30 says He can be grieved, and grief is an emotion. We know the Holy Spirit has a will because 1 Corinthians 12:11 tells us the Holy Spirit distributes spiritual gifts "to each one individually as he wills." The Holy Spirit has a mind, emotions, and a will, so does that sound like a mere force to you, or does it sound more like a person?

JEHOVAH'S WITNESS: Hmm…interesting.

CHRISTIAN: We also know that the Holy Spirit does things that only a person can do. John 14:26 says He teaches believers. John 15:26 says He testifies to the truth. In Acts 13:4 He commissioned people to service. In Acts 8:29 He issued a command to believers. Romans 8:27 says He prays for believers. An impersonal force cannot do these kinds of things. Only a person can.

JEHOVAH'S WITNESS: Okay.

CHRISTIAN: The Holy Spirit is also treated like a person. For example, Acts 5:3 indicates that Ananias and Sapphira were guilty of lying to the Holy Spirit. Can you lie to a force? [Smile.] You'd think I was crazy if I confessed to you that I lied to my electricity early this morning, wouldn't you?

JEHOVAH'S WITNESS: Ha ha. Can't deny that.

CHRISTIAN: The Holy Spirit can also be obeyed. Acts 13:2 records a command of the Holy Spirit that Paul and Barnabas obeyed. A force, by contrast, cannot be obeyed. [Smile.] Again, you'd think I was nuts if I told you my electricity commanded me to do some things today, right?

JEHOVAH'S WITNESS: [Smiling.]

CHRISTIAN: Well, all kidding aside, those are the reasons I think the Holy Spirit is a person and not a force.

JEHOVAH'S WITNESS: Okay. I understand your position. But I still see no evidence that the Holy Spirit is God.

CHRISTIAN: Okay. Let's look at that. For one thing, Acts 5:3-4 equates lying to the Holy Spirit and lying to God. Also, 2 Corinthians

3:17-18 refers to the Holy Spirit as "the Lord," a term elsewhere used of Jehovah. The Holy Spirit is often referred to as the "Spirit of God," thus indicating His full deity. As well, He has all the attributes of deity. For example, Psalm 139:7 indicates the Holy Spirit is everywhere-present. First Corinthians 2:10 indicates the Holy Spirit is all-knowing. Romans 15:19 indicates the Holy Spirit is all-powerful. Hebrews 9:14 indicates the Holy Spirit is eternal. I could go on and on, but the point is, Scripture identifies the Holy Spirit as not just a person, but also as God.

JEHOVAH'S WITNESS: Okay, well I'd need to look at those verses.

CHRISTIAN: I'll write them down for you before you leave. It'll only take me a moment.

JEHOVAH'S WITNESS: Okay.

CHRISTIAN: I know all this can be a bit daunting. I hope this isn't overwhelming to you. I certainly commend you for your search for spiritual truth. If we could, why don't we forget that I'm a Bible-church Christian and you're a Jehovah's Witness, and for a moment just consider ourselves to be two human beings in search of spiritual truth. Let's keep meeting and let's keep talking. Are you game? Can we set a date and a topic for our next discussion?

Conversation Highlights

Allow me to highlight a few tactical points from this conversation.

- Instead of waiting for the Jehovah's Witness to launch into his chosen topic of discussion, I asked the first question and steered the conversation from the start.

- I followed my traditional approach of challenging the accuracy of the Watchtower Society while correcting at least one major doctrine.

- I offered to provide documentation for some of my assertions.

- I not only answered objections raised against the personhood of the Holy Spirit but also presented a positive case for it.

- I closed the discussion by trying to disarm any resistance so the other person would be willing to meet again.

- I invited him to set a date and a topic so I could be prepared.

Digging Deeper

You may be interested in more in-depth information on the Jehovah's Witnesses' view of the Holy Spirit and the specific Bible verses they cite to support it. If so, I invite you to consult my book *Reasoning from the Scriptures with the Jehovah's Witnesses* (2009 edition), pages 195–216.

17

Conversations About the Trinity

———∞∞∞———

The Watchtower Society teaches that if people were to read the Bible from Genesis to Revelation without any preconceived ideas, they would never arrive at a belief in the Trinity. Instead they would consistently find the belief that God is one.[1] The doctrine of the Trinity, they say, is a man-made invention.

Watchtower literature refers to "the unreasonable and unscriptural doctrine of the Trinity—three Gods in one person."[2] The Watchtower also sometimes describes the Trinity as a freakish being.

> When the clergy are asked by their followers as to how such a combination of three in one can possibly exist, they are obliged to answer, "That is a mystery." Some will try to illustrate it by using triangles, trefoils, or images with three heads on one neck. Nevertheless, sincere persons who want to know the true God and serve him find it a bit difficult to love and worship a complicated, freakish-looking, three-headed God.[3]

Satan, the father of lies, is viewed as the true originator of the doctrine of the Trinity. "Never was there a more deceptive doctrine advanced than that of the Trinity. It could have originated only in one mind, and that the mind of Satan the Devil."[4] Further, Jehovah's Witnesses claim the doctrine is rooted in paganism. Indeed, in the centuries preceding the time of Christ, there were trinities of gods predominant in such pagan cultures as ancient Babylonia, Egypt, and Assyria. "Under the guise of Christianity, Christendom teaches doctrines—including the Trinity...that are awash in myths and falsehoods...By heeding God's warning to separate ourselves and 'quit touching the unclean thing,' we will not be misled by false stories."[5] At some point, this doctrine allegedly infiltrated the early Christian church.

Jehovah's Witnesses add, "It is worth noting that the word 'Trinity' never occurs in the Bible."[6] If the word is not in the Bible, it cannot possibly represent a biblical doctrine.

One should be aware that throughout its history, the Watchtower Society has falsely caricatured the doctrine of the Trinity in order to make its denial of the doctrine seem more plausible to reasonable people. In *Studies in the Scriptures* (1899), for example, the doctrine is defined as "three Gods in one God."[7] Of course, Trinitarians do not believe in "three Gods in one God," but rather three co-equal persons in the one Godhead.

Falsehoods to Watch For

- The doctrine of the Trinity entails belief in three Gods in one God.

- One would never derive the doctrine of the Trinity by reading straight through the Bible.

- The doctrine of the Trinity is man-made and is inspired by the devil.

- The doctrine of the Trinity is rooted in paganism.

- Because the word "Trinity" is not in the Bible, it cannot represent a biblical doctrine.

Important Points to Introduce

- The doctrine of the Trinity entails belief in three persons in one God.

- Reading the Bible from Genesis to Revelation reveals (1) there is one God; (2) three persons are called God in the Bible—the Father, the Son, and the Holy Spirit; and (3) there is three-in-oneness in God.

- Though the word "Trinity" is not in the Bible, the doctrine of the Trinity is a clear biblical inference based on the explicit teachings of the Bible.

- The doctrine of the Trinity is not man-made, not inspired by the devil, and not rooted in paganism.

Eavesdropping on a Conversation

JEHOVAH'S WITNESS: Good afternoon. I hope I didn't catch you at a bad time. My colleague and I are Jehovah's Witnesses, and we're making the rounds in your neighborhood today. Can we talk a few minutes?

CHRISTIAN: Sure, no problem. But before you begin, can I ask you whether you intend to talk to me about conclusions you have come to as a result of reading the Bible alone without any outside helps, or will you be passing on to me what you've been told the Bible means by the Watchtower Society? [Silently pray the open-the-heart prayer.]

JEHOVAH'S WITNESS: Well, I do read the Bible, but I have come to understand the Bible through Jehovah's organization, the Watchtower Society.

CHRISTIAN: Have you ever read the entire Bible all the way through?

JEHOVAH'S WITNESS: Well, I'm working on it.

CHRISTIAN: [Smile.] I take that as a no.

JEHOVAH'S WITNESS: Yes, but ask me that question in another year or two, and you'll probably get a different answer.

CHRISTIAN: Okay. Well, let me ask you this. As a Jehovah's Witness, are you instructed to read only Watchtower publications in coming to understand the Bible, or are you also allowed to consult non-Watchtower books, such as Bible commentaries written by other Christians?

JEHOVAH'S WITNESS: No, we read only Watchtower books. But there's a good reason for that. Many Bible commentaries and other such books are actually part of an apostate Satan-inspired Christendom that can lead you astray.

CHRISTIAN: Was it the Watchtower Society that taught you that?

JEHOVAH'S WITNESS: Yes.

CHRISTIAN: So the Watchtower Society instructed you that only Watchtower materials are trustworthy and that you can surely trust these materials because the Watchtower Society told you so?

JEHOVAH'S WITNESS: The Watchtower Society is God's mouthpiece on earth.

CHRISTIAN: [Smile.] I understand that you believe that. But do you take their word at everything they say, or do you have the freedom to ever question it?

JEHOVAH'S WITNESS: A person shouldn't question the Watchtower Society because that amounts to questioning Jehovah.

CHRISTIAN: Am I right in saying that you don't question the Watchtower Society because the Watchtower Society told you not to question it?

JEHOVAH'S WITNESS: Well, that's true. But I also don't question it because it is Jehovah's organization.

CHRISTIAN: Did Jehovah Himself tell you that the Watchtower Society is the voice of Jehovah on earth, or did the Watchtower Society itself tell you that?

JEHOVAH'S WITNESS: Jehovah has never spoken to me personally. He speaks only through the Watchtower Society.

CHRISTIAN: Am I right in saying that if you do question the Watchtower Society, you can get kicked out and your Jehovah's Witness friends won't talk to you?

JEHOVAH'S WITNESS: We can be disfellowshipped and shunned, yes.

CHRISTIAN: That makes me wonder if you ever question Watchtower teachings in your heart without verbalizing such doubts to anyone. That's not a question. I just wonder about it.

JEHOVAH'S WITNESS: Well, I believe the Watchtower Society is God's organization, and for that reason I don't question it.

CHRISTIAN: One thing that concerns me about this is that if I believe that the Bible teaches a particular doctrine, and then the

Watchtower Society tells me not to believe that doctrine, I'm forced to go against something I believe to be true and to submit my mind to an organization that didn't even come into existence until the late nineteenth century.

JEHOVAH'S WITNESS: What kind of doctrine are you talking about?

CHRISTIAN: Well, for example, I believe in the doctrine of the Trinity, but I understand that the Watchtower Society rejects it. Am I right?

JEHOVAH'S WITNESS: That is correct.

CHRISTIAN: Can I ask you what led you to believe that the doctrine of the Trinity is false?

JEHOVAH'S WITNESS: The doctrine of the Trinity is rooted in paganism. It might surprise you to learn that the word "Trinity" is not even in the Bible. That means there's no way it can be a biblical doctrine.

CHRISTIAN: I'm not sure that's a sound argument. After all, haven't the Jehovah's Witnesses—and especially the Watchtower Society—claimed to be a theocracy, that is, a God-ruled organization?

JEHOVAH'S WITNESS: Well, that's true.

CHRISTIAN: The word "theocracy" is not in the Bible. So if we're going to reject the Trinity because the word isn't in the Bible, shouldn't we reject the idea of a theocracy since that word is not in the Bible either?

JEHOVAH'S WITNESS: Okay, I see your point.

CHRISTIAN: By the way, did you know that theocracies existed in pagan cultures, like Rome? But simply because Rome had a form of theocracy does not mean that all theocracies are pagan, right? After all, Israel was a theocracy too.

JEHOVAH'S WITNESS: Fair enough. Good point.

CHRISTIAN: Even though the word "Trinity" is not in the Bible, I believe the concept of the Trinity is a biblical one. Can I tell you why I believe that?

JEHOVAH'S WITNESS: Okay.

CHRISTIAN: The doctrine of the Trinity is based on three lines of evidence. First, the Bible is absolutely clear that there is only one God. The fact that there is only one true God is the consistent testimony of Scripture from Genesis to Revelation. It is like a thread that runs through every page of the Bible. You'd agree with me so far, right?

JEHOVAH'S WITNESS: So far so good.

CHRISTIAN: Good. Second, however, the Bible also indicates that the Father is God, the Son is God, and the Holy Spirit is God. For example, 1 Peter 1:2 says the Father is God. Hebrews 1:8 says Jesus is God. Acts 5:3-4 indicates that the Holy Spirit is God. I can write these verses down for you before you leave. And third, the Bible indicates that there is three-in-oneness in God. For example, we are told in Matthew 28:19 to baptize in the name of the Father and the Son and the Holy Spirit. Are you following me so far?

JEHOVAH'S WITNESS: I understand what you're saying.

CHRISTIAN: Okay, good. Now, Matthew 28:19 is particularly important. Notice again that it says we are to baptize people "in the name of the Father and of the Son and of the Holy Spirit." The word "name" is singular in the Greek, indicating one God. But notice the definite article—the word "the"—before Father, Son, and Holy Spirit. Bible scholars say that indicates distinct persons. There's one God, but three distinct persons within the one God.

JEHOVAH'S WITNESS: Hmm…I'm not sure about that.

CHRISTIAN: Okay. Perhaps it might help if I put it in the form of a question. If I believe in everything that Scripture says about a particular issue, and I use a term to describe it that isn't in the Bible, am I being more faithful to Scripture than someone who uses only terms found in the Bible but rejects clear aspects of God's revelation?

JEHOVAH'S WITNESS: I've never heard it put that way. But I still feel that if a person were to read the Bible straight through from Genesis to Revelation, he would never come up with the doctrine of the Trinity.

CHRISTIAN: But I've read most of the Old and New Testaments, and I've come to the conclusion that the doctrine of the Trinity is true.

JEHOVAH'S WITNESS: The primary emphasis of the Bible is that God is one. There's always been one true God.

CHRISTIAN: You believe that this one true God is Jehovah, and He is the Father, right?

JEHOVAH'S WITNESS: Right.

CHRISTIAN: He is the one true God?

JEHOVAH'S WITNESS: Yes.

CHRISTIAN: Would you agree that whatever is not true must be false?

JEHOVAH'S WITNESS: I suppose so.

CHRISTIAN: If there is only one true God, all other gods must be false gods, right?

JEHOVAH'S WITNESS: Okay.

CHRISTIAN: Well, you believe John 1:1 teaches that Jesus is a god, right?

JEHOVAH'S WITNESS: Yes.

CHRISTIAN: So, is Jesus a true god or a false god?

JEHOVAH'S WITNESS: Hmm...I'm not sure about that.

CHRISTIAN: Jesus can't be a false god because that would make the Watchtower understanding of John 1:1 incorrect. Therefore Jesus must be a true God. But as you said, Jehovah is the only true God. If Jehovah is the only true God, and if Jesus is a true God, then Jesus must be Jehovah, just as the Father is. If you disagree with this, can you demonstrate to me why it is wrong?

JEHOVAH'S WITNESS: Hmm...I'm going to have to think about all this. But it sounds like you believe in three Gods in one God.

CHRISTIAN: Actually Christians don't believe in three Gods in one God. We both reject that understanding of the Trinity. As a Trinitarian, I believe there is only one true God, but within the perfect unity of God are three co-equal and co-eternal persons—the Father, the Son, and the Holy Spirit.

JEHOVAH'S WITNESS: That just doesn't make sense to us.

CHRISTIAN: The way I see it, it would not make sense to say there are three Gods in one God. But it does not violate reason to say there are three persons in the one God. Look at it this way. In the Trinity there are three *whos* in one *what*.

JEHOVAH'S WITNESS: I don't know about that. This three-in-one idea is clearly seen in pagan cultures, such as Babylon and Assyria. These pagan cultures believed in trinities of gods. There is good reason to say that the doctrine of the Trinity is inspired by the devil. At some point, this pagan idea infiltrated the early church.

CHRISTIAN: Actually I've done a bit of study on this issue. I had heard that there were some religious groups who claimed the Trinity was rooted in paganism. What I discovered is that these pagan cultures did not believe in trinities. Rather, they believed in triads of gods who headed up pantheons of many other gods. But these triads constituted three separate gods. This is completely different from the doctrine of the Trinity, which says there is only one God with three persons in the one God.

JEHOVAH'S WITNESS: But that's such a confusing concept of God. First Corinthians 14:33 tells us that God is not a God of confusion. Because the doctrine of the Trinity is a confusing doctrine, it seems impossible that it could be true.

CHRISTIAN: In my thinking, simply because a person is not able to fully comprehend a doctrine does not mean that doctrine is false. I don't understand all the physics behind the law of gravity, but I'm quite sure that if I jump off a cliff, I'll fall. In other words, I believe the law of gravity is true even though I don't understand all of it. I likewise believe in the Trinity even though I don't fully understand everything about it. The way I look at it, for human beings to be able to understand everything about God, they would need to have the very mind of God.

JEHOVAH'S WITNESS: I don't deny that. But 1 Corinthians 14:33 says God is not a God of confusion.

CHRISTIAN: [Smile.] Well, actually that verse has nothing to do with the Trinity. In context, the Corinthian church was plagued by internal divisions and disorder, especially in regard to the public exercise of certain spiritual gifts, such as prophesying. Paul said that since God is not a God of confusion, the church ought to model itself after God by avoiding disharmony in its services—such as the disharmony that erupts when lots of people prophesy at the same time. So Paul first tells the Corinthian believers that only two or three prophets should speak in any given service and that only one should speak at a time. He then states the underlying principle of these instructions: "God is not a God of confusion but of peace." Seen in this light, this verse is completely unrelated to the Trinity.

JEHOVAH'S WITNESS: I've not heard that before. I'll have to give it some thought.

CHRISTIAN: Well, in any event, I know all this can be a bit daunting. I do commend you for your commitment to finding the truth. Before you make a final decision on the doctrine of the Trinity, why not commit to making an informed decision? Doesn't that seem reasonable?

JEHOVAH'S WITNESS: That sounds reasonable, but what do you mean?

CHRISTIAN: What I mean is, let's be like the Bereans in Acts 17:11 who tested everything the apostle Paul said against Scripture. Paul didn't get mad at them when they did this. In fact, Paul commended them. So just as the Bereans tested Paul's teachings by measuring them against the Bible, both of us can test all things—including the teachings of my church and the teachings of the Watchtower Society—by measuring them against the Bible alone. After all, the Bible came directly from Jehovah. The Watchtower Society began in the late nineteenth century. By studying the Bible alone, I think you may gain an entirely different perspective on the doctrine of the Trinity.

JEHOVAH'S WITNESS: Well, I'm not sure. I'll think about it.

CHRISTIAN: Okay, good. There is one more thing. I imagine you use a Bible published by the Watchtower Society—the New World Translation. In order to genuinely test the teachings of the Watchtower Society, would you consider measuring their teachings against a Bible not published by the Watchtower Society? I can assure you from personal experience that the New American Standard Bible, the English Standard Version, the New International

Version, and the New Living Translation are good translations. I've used these translations for years, and they're all very reliable.

JEHOVAH'S WITNESS: Well, I'll give it some thought.

CHRISTIAN: Can we meet again? How 'bout we set a date?

Conversation Highlights

Allow me to highlight a few points from this conversation.

- As I did in the last few chapters, in this conversation I was the aggressor in asking the first question and directing the conversation.

- Throughout the conversation, I challenged the trustworthiness of the Watchtower Society and corrected its teaching about the Trinity.

- I answered objections to the Trinity and presented a positive case for it.

- When I sensed the Jehovah's Witness was still somewhat resistant to what I was saying about the Trinity, I responded, "Before you make a final decision on the doctrine of the Trinity, why not commit to making an informed decision?" This strategy opened the door for the discussion to continue.

- At the end of the conversation, I challenged the Jehovah's Witness to test the Watchtower Society against Scripture, using a reliable translation.

- I closed by inviting the Jehovah's Witness to set a date for the next visit.

Digging Deeper

You may be interested in more in-depth information on Jehovah's Witnesses' view of the Trinity and the specific Bible verses they cite to support it. If so, I invite you to consult my book *Reasoning from the Scriptures with the Jehovah's Witnesses* (2009 edition), pages 217–252.

Conversations About the Anointed Class and Other Sheep

⸻ ∞∞∞ ⸻

Watchtower theology distinguishes between two different groups of saved people with two different destinies and sets of privileges. Highest privileges go to the Anointed Class—144,000 Jehovah's Witnesses who will allegedly experience a heavenly destiny (Revelation 7:4; 14:1-3). Because they are so few, Jesus referred to them as the "little flock" (Luke 12:32). It first emerged with the 12 apostles and other Christians in the first century.

The Watchtower teaches that "God has purposed to associate a limited number of faithful humans with Jesus Christ in the heavenly Kingdom."[1] Only members of the Anointed Class are born again, thereby becoming sons of God and heirs with Christ (see John 1:12-13; Romans 8:16-17). Only these are privileged to partake of the Lord's Supper (1 Corinthians 11:20-29). These alone experience a spiritual (that is, nonphysical) existence in heaven.

This group of 144,000 was reportedly filled by around 1935. "The heavenly hope was held out, highlighted, and stressed until about the year 1935. Then as 'light flashed up' to reveal clearly the identity of the 'great crowd' of Revelation 7:9 [that is, Jehovah's Witnesses who are not of the Anointed Class], the emphasis began to be placed on the earthly hope."[2]

This means that all Jehovah's Witnesses who have lived since 1935 will not experience a heavenly, spiritual destiny, as will the Anointed Class, but rather will inherit eternal life as physical beings in an earthly paradise. These are the "other sheep" Jesus referred to in John 10:16. Jehovah has given the earth to humankind, and here these other sheep—the great multitude—will dwell for all eternity (see Psalm 37:9,11,29). Their hope is to survive end-time calamities, including the approaching great tribulation and Armageddon, and then dwell in the earthly paradise Jehovah will provide. The other sheep who have died will be resurrected to enjoy earthly blessings.

The 144,000 Jehovah's Witnesses who make up the Anointed Class will rule with Christ over the other sheep, who will be on earth.[3] These 144,000 "will be priests of God and of Christ, and they will reign with him for a thousand years" (Revelation 20:6). They are apparently Jehovah's elite.

Falsehoods to Watch For

- God has two classes of true followers.
- The Anointed Class—made up of 144,000 privileged Jehovah's Witnesses—experience a spiritual existence in heaven and rule with Christ.
- The other sheep—all other Jehovah's Witnesses—will live forever in an earthly paradise in subjection to Christ and the 144,000 members of the Anointed Class.

Important Points to Introduce

- There is only one people of God.
- All people of God share one destiny.
- All of God's people enjoy the same privileges.

Eavesdropping on a Conversation

JEHOVAH'S WITNESS: Good morning. We attend the local Kingdom Hall and would appreciate a few minutes of your time.

CHRISTIAN: Okay. So, you're Jehovah's Witnesses, right? [Silently pray the open-the-heart prayer.]

JEHOVAH'S WITNESS: Yes. With the world as it is today, many people are crying out for answers. It seems like nations are rising against nations in war, famine is on the rise, the crime rate has never been higher, the economy is hurting countless people, and things seem to be getting worse by the day. Do you think that Jehovah will one day intervene and solve the problems of humankind? Do you think that Jehovah will ever establish a paradise on earth for humankind?

CHRISTIAN: Well, I think He will. But I think that much of what we are seeing today was actually predicted by the biblical prophets in regard to the end times. And—please take no offense—but it seems to me that the Jehovah's Witnesses have set forth quite a few prophecies that never came to pass, so that raises red flags in my mind.

JEHOVAH'S WITNESS: Okay. Well, what prophecies are you referring to?

CHRISTIAN: Well, the Watchtower predicted that in 1914, Jehovah would overthrow all human governments and fully establish His kingdom on earth. In 1925, select Old Testament saints, such as Abraham, Isaac, and Jacob, were to rise from the grave and live in San Diego. In 1975 human history was to end. None of those things happened.

JEHOVAH'S WITNESS: Yes, all that is quite regretful. We are aware that we've made mistakes. We were wrong on those dates. And on behalf of Jehovah's Witnesses, I want to apologize to you for those mistaken dates. Will you forgive us?

CHRISTIAN: Wow, I've never heard a Jehovah's Witness apologize for its organization's false prophecies. That's mighty kind. And of course I forgive you.

JEHOVAH'S WITNESS: We're appreciative. Thanks.

CHRISTIAN: No problem. You know, I'm impressed with your apology. And I appreciate that you offered it. I really do. But I've got to ask you something—and again, please take no offense. My question is this. Where does the Bible say that if a false prophet apologizes for his false prophecies, he is no longer a false prophet? Have you ever thought about that?

JEHOVAH'S WITNESS: Well, I'm not sure how to respond.

CHRISTIAN: Well, this is such an important and foundational issue. I really mean it when I say that I appreciate your apology on behalf of the Jehovah's Witnesses. But the truth is, that really doesn't change the status of the Watchtower Society as a false prophet, does it?

JEHOVAH'S WITNESS: Well, I see your point. But since the days of those wrong dates, our leaders have received new light and have a much sharper perspective on things.

CHRISTIAN: But that doesn't change the Watchtower's status as an organization that has announced false prophecies.

JEHOVAH'S WITNESS: I understand your feelings.

CHRISTIAN: And this "new light" doctrine has some other problems as well. It implies that as time continues to pass, the light gets ever brighter. That seems to imply that maybe twenty years from now, the new light of that future day will negate what Jehovah's Witnesses presently believe. Tell me, do you think truth changes over the years, or is it simply that the Watchtower Society got it wrong?

JEHOVAH'S WITNESS: Well, we've admitted our mistakes and continue to seek to bring Jehovah's message to people around the world.

CHRISTIAN: Speaking of people around the world, doesn't the Watchtower teach that there are two peoples of God—one with a destiny in heaven and one with a destiny on earth?

JEHOVAH'S WITNESS: That's correct. There are 144,000 Jehovah's Witnesses who will experience a heavenly destiny, and these are called the Anointed Class. This group first emerged with the twelve apostles and other Christians in the first century. They will have a spiritual existence in heaven alongside Christ, and they will reign with him. The full number of the 144,000 was met in 1935.

CHRISTIAN: Well, if only 144,000 are to have a heavenly destiny, this makes me wonder how there could be any available slots by the time the Watchtower Society was founded in the late nineteenth century. After all, there were hundreds of thousands of believers in the early church, beginning in the book of Acts, and many of these became martyrs. Surely they would have been among the 144,000. That, along with all the other conversions until the late nineteenth century, would seem to mean no Jehovah's Witnesses at all could be among the group.

JEHOVAH'S WITNESS: Well, many Jehovah's Witnesses are a part of the group.

CHRISTIAN: It seems to me that a big problem with the idea that pre-1935 Jehovah's Witnesses are among the 144,000 is that what they believed is now considered by the Watchtower Society to be pagan. For example, in those early years, it was taught by the Watchtower that Christ died on a cross, not on a stake. It was taught that Jesus was worshipped, not just shown obeisance. Back in those early days they were allowed to celebrate Christmas and birthdays, unlike today. How could Jehovah's Witnesses with such alleged pagan beliefs be a part of the 144,000?

JEHOVAH'S WITNESS: Ah…I've never thought about that before. That indeed is a good point.

CHRISTIAN: Anyway, who is the other group?

JEHOVAH'S WITNESS: These are what we call the "other sheep," and they will live forever in an earthly paradise. We all hope to survive the calamities prophesied of the end times and dwell in this new paradise that Jehovah will provide.

CHRISTIAN: What is the scriptural support for the idea that there are two different peoples of God?

JEHOVAH'S WITNESS: Well, there are verses that make the distinction. For example, the New World Translation renders Revelation 7:4, "And I heard the number of those who were sealed, a hundred and forty-four thousand, sealed out of every tribe of the sons of Israel." This is the Anointed Class of Jehovah's Witnesses. The book of Revelation actually refers to the 144,000 as the twelve tribes of Israel, but that's actually a metaphorical reference to the Anointed Class.

CHRISTIAN: Why do you say it is a metaphor? What led you to that conclusion?

JEHOVAH'S WITNESS: Well, Ephraim and Dan were tribes of Israel in the Old Testament, but they aren't included in the list in Revelation 7.

So the list in Revelation 7 must not be meant to be taken literally. As well, the Levites are in the list of Revelation 7, but in the Old Testament, the Levites were set apart for priestly duty and weren't reckoned as one of the twelve tribes. So again, the list in Revelation 7 must be metaphorical.

CHRISTIAN: I think I understand your view. Have you ever considered the possibility that Revelation 7 is referring to the actual twelve tribes of Israel but that adjustments were made regarding the specific tribes mentioned?

JEHOVAH'S WITNESS: I can't imagine why that would be so.

CHRISTIAN: Well, first of all, every other reference in the Bible to the twelve tribes of Israel always refers to twelve tribes of Israel. In fact, the word "tribes" is never used of anything but a literal ethnic group in Scripture. So, why should Revelation 7 be interpreted as metaphorical?

JEHOVAH'S WITNESS: Hmm…Well, that's our view.

CHRISTIAN: Here's something else to think about. The Watchtower Society interprets the twelve tribes metaphorically, but it interprets the number 144,000 literally. So really, the Watchtower Society takes both a metaphorical *and* a literal approach to the same verse. Does this combined approach sound legit to you? It seems like a real stretch to me.

JEHOVAH'S WITNESS: Okay. That's an interesting observation.

CHRISTIAN: I just noticed something else. Revelation 14:4 says that each of these 144,000 are men who have never been defiled with women. This would seem to exclude all women from the Anointed Class. What do you make of that?

JEHOVAH'S WITNESS: Wow. I'm really not sure. I never noticed that verse before.

CHRISTIAN: Now that I think about it, I think there are some good reasons why the tribes of Dan and Ephraim are not mentioned in the list of tribes in Revelation 7. First, the Old Testament contains about twenty lists of tribes, and they aren't all identical. Dan's tribe was probably omitted in Revelation because that tribe was guilty of idolatry on many occasions and, as a result, was largely obliterated. Ephraim's tribe, too, was involved in idolatry and paganized worship. So wouldn't it make sense to you that these two tribes would not be mentioned in the list of tribes in Revelation 7?

JEHOVAH'S WITNESS: Well, I guess that's possible. But what about the inclusion of the tribe of Levi?

CHRISTIAN: According to the book of Hebrews, when Christ our high priest appeared on the scene, the priestly functions of the tribe of Levi ceased. The Levitical priesthood was replaced by Christ's. Because there was no further need for the services of the tribe of Levi as priests, there was no further reason for keeping this tribe distinct and separate from the others, so they were properly included in the tribal listing in the book of Revelation. So in my thinking, there's no good reason for interpreting the twelve tribes in Revelation 7 metaphorically.

JEHOVAH'S WITNESS: If the 144,000 are not the Anointed Class, then who are the other sheep Jesus spoke of in John 10:16?

CHRISTIAN: That's a good question. Notice that the Gospels refer to "the lost sheep of Israel." These are lost Jews who needed to be redeemed by Christ. We see this, for example, in Matthew 10:6. When these Jews became believers in Christ, they became His sheep, according to John 10. When Jesus refers to other sheep from a different sheepfold, He is referring to Gentile believers as opposed to Jewish believers. In John 10:16, Jesus affirms that the Gentile and Jewish believers will make up one flock with one shepherd—not one flock on earth and one flock in heaven.

JEHOVAH'S WITNESS: That's a lot to digest. I'm going to have to look into what the Watchtower has to say about all this.

CHRISTIAN: I hope you do look further into this. But I think you should make the Bible your barometer of truth. The Watchtower Society has been wrong too many times regarding too many doctrines for it to be the end-all determiner of religious truth. The Bible alone is the Word of God.

JEHOVAH'S WITNESS: Well, hmm...

CHRISTIAN: One thing you'll find, as you examine the Bible alone, is that all believers in Christ have a destiny in heaven. In Philippians 3:20-21 all Christians are called citizens of heaven. First Thessalonians 4:13-17 says that all Christians look forward to eternally being with the Lord in heaven. First Peter 1:3-5 says we all have an inheritance waiting for us in heaven. Hebrews 11:8-10 says we're all headed for the heavenly country. Never is heaven restricted to 144,000 alone. I want to write these verses down for you so you'll be able to study them on your own, okay? Then we can talk about them the next time you come by. Before you go, though, can I tell you why I'm sure that if I die today I'll go straight to heaven? [If the Jehovah's Witness says yes, share the gospel of grace and plenty of joyful testimony. (See chapter 19, "Conversations About Salvation.") Then ask if he'd like to trust in Christ alone for the gift of eternal life, thus guaranteeing his place in heaven. Be sure to set a date for the next meeting.]

Conversation Highlights

Allow me to highlight a few tactical points from this conversation.

- As in some previous conversations, I transitioned from a topic of lesser importance (the dire state of affairs in the world) to a topic of greater importance (the claim that there are two peoples of God).

- I followed my standard approach of challenging the trustworthiness of the Watchtower Society while at the same time correcting at least one major doctrine.

- Notice that the Jehovah's Witness apologized for the Watchtower's false prophecies. Whenever they do this, accept the apology, but don't allow them to marginalize the reality that the Watchtower Society remains a false prophet.

- I gently debunked their "new light" comeback.

- I sought to answer their objections and present a positive case for the idea that there is one people of God.

- I gave a brief testimony and shared the gospel of grace, followed by an invitation to trust in Christ alone for eternal life.
- I requested a date for another visit.

Digging Deeper

You may be interested in more in-depth information on the Jehovah's Witnesses' view of two peoples of God and the specific Bible verses they cite to support it. If so, I invite you to consult my book *Reasoning from the Scriptures with the Jehovah's Witnesses* (2009 edition), pages 253–282.

19

Conversations About Salvation

———◦◦◦———

Biblical Christians speak of salvation as being by grace alone through faith alone. Nothing else is added into the mix. Jehovah's Witnesses claim to believe in salvation by grace through faith, but they actually believe in a salvation by works. They believe total obedience to the Watchtower Society is necessary in order to attain salvation. Good works play a pivotal role. They interpret Philippians 2:12 in a works context, which in the New World Translation reads, "Consequently, my beloved ones, in the way that you have always obeyed, not during my presence only, but now much more readily during my absence, keep working out your own salvation with fear and trembling." The only way to work out one's salvation, they say, is by engaging in good works. Indeed, "to get one's name written in that Book of Life will depend upon one's works."[1] One must continually be "working hard for the reward of eternal life."[2]

A Jehovah's Witness named Melanie informed me that working out her salvation included going door to door and handing out Watchtower literature. Some Jehovah's Witnesses spend a hundred hours each month handing out literature on doorsteps and leading home Bible studies.

There is no assurance of salvation in Watchtower theology. The typical Jehovah's Witness hopes that his or her unbending stance against sin and complete obedience to the Watchtower Society will be enough, but one cannot be sure.

Not only that, but obedience in the present life is not enough. Jehovah's Witnesses must also render complete obedience during the future millennium. Only if the Jehovah's Witness faithfully serves Jehovah during this 1000-year period will he be granted final salvation. Should one fail, he will be annihilated.

Because of this heavy emphasis on works and obedience to the Watchtower Society, Jesus's work of salvation in His death plays a relatively minor role. Jehovah's Witnesses claim that the human life Jesus laid down in sacrifice was exactly equal to the human life Adam fell with. "Since one man's sin (that of Adam) had been responsible for causing the entire human family to be sinners, the shed blood of another perfect human...being of corresponding value, could balance the scales of justice."[3] Jesus died *as a man* for the sin inherited from another man (Adam).

In view of this salvation by works, one naturally wonders how Jehovah's Witnesses can claim that salvation is a free gift received by grace. Former Jehovah's Witness Duane Magnani sheds light on the matter.

> What the Watchtower means by "free gift" is that Christ's death only wiped away the sin inherited from Adam. They teach that without this work of atonement, men could not work their way toward salvation. But the "gift" of Christ's ransom sacrifice is freely made available to all who desire it. In other words, without Christ's sacrifice, the individual wouldn't have a chance to get saved. But in view of His work, the free gift which removed the sin inherited from Adam, the individual now has a chance.[4]

Falsehoods to Watch For

- Salvation is based on works and involves total obedience to the Watchtower.

- Distributing Watchtower literature door to door is pivotal in the process.

- One cannot be sure of salvation in this life.

- Jesus's work of salvation on the cross is downplayed. The human life Jesus laid down in sacrifice is exactly equal to the human life Adam fell with.

- Salvation is called a free gift, but the gift is only that the sin inherited from Adam has been wiped away, and people now have the opportunity to work out their own salvation.

Important Points to Introduce

- Salvation is based on grace alone through faith alone.

- Jesus attained a complete redemption for us by His death on the cross.

- One can have an assurance of salvation in this life.

- Works are not the condition of our salvation, but a consequence of it. We are saved not by works, but by the kind of faith that produces works.

Eavesdropping on a Conversation

JEHOVAH'S WITNESS: Good afternoon. Did I catch you at a bad time?

CHRISTIAN: No. Can I help you?

JEHOVAH'S WITNESS: We're visiting today from the local Kingdom Hall over on Main Street. We are Jehovah's Witnesses and would love to chat if you have a minute.

CHRISTIAN: Okay. [Silently pray the open-the-heart prayer.]

JEHOVAH'S WITNESS: One of the concerns we have is that many of today's modern churches have bought into the idea that all people have to do is believe in Jesus, and they will go to heaven regardless of what kind of life that they have lived.

CHRISTIAN: Well, most Christian churches do teach that salvation is by grace through faith.

JEHOVAH'S WITNESS: Have you considered Philippians 2:12? The New World Translation renders the verse this way: "Consequently, my beloved ones, in the way that you have always obeyed, not during my presence only, but now much more readily during my absence, keep working out your own salvation with fear and trembling."

The only way a person can work out his or her salvation is by doing the kinds of works that Jehovah speaks of in the Bible. In fact, we believe it is an ongoing process. We must continually be about the business of working out our salvation before Jehovah by good works.

CHRISTIAN: So you don't believe in salvation by grace?

JEHOVAH'S WITNESS: We actually do. But we think many Christians and many churches have misinterpreted the doctrine of grace. Can I tell you Jehovah's view on the matter?

CHRISTIAN: [Smile.] I'm all ears.

JEHOVAH'S WITNESS: Salvation is indeed by grace. It is a free gift. What we mean by this is that Christ's death wiped away the sin inherited from Adam. Without this gracious work of Christ, there is no way any of us would have a chance to work out our salvation. The gift of Christ's ransom sacrifice is made freely available to all people. Because of this gift, we have the opportunity to engage in works that can lead to salvation.

CHRISTIAN: With that kind of definition of grace, it doesn't sound to me like anyone can be sure whether they're saved. Do you believe a person can become assured that he or she is saved?

JEHOVAH'S WITNESS: We can be assured that if we stand against sin and obey the Watchtower Society, we will be saved.

CHRISTIAN: How do you know whether you've done enough good works to earn your salvation?

JEHOVAH'S WITNESS: Well, your lack of knowing how much is enough serves as a motivation to continued faithfulness.

CHRISTIAN: Why do I have to obey the Watchtower Society to be saved?

JEHOVAH'S WITNESS: The Watchtower Society is Jehovah's mouthpiece on earth. Without this organization, no one on earth could understand the Bible.

CHRISTIAN: When did the Watchtower Society first come into being?

JEHOVAH'S WITNESS: The Watchtower Society was founded in the late nineteenth century.

CHRISTIAN: So, what about people who lived prior to that time? Obviously, since the Watchtower Society did not exist, these people were unable to obey the rules of the Watchtower Society. Were none of them saved?

JEHOVAH'S WITNESS: Only those obedient to Jehovah were saved.

CHRISTIAN: [Smile.] If people back then could be saved without the Watchtower Society, why can't people do the same today?

JEHOVAH'S WITNESS: This is what Jehovah has taught us today through the Watchtower Society. We are called to obey Jehovah's voice as expressed through the Watchtower Society.

CHRISTIAN: It sounds to me like the Watchtower Society has marginalized Christ's work of salvation in His death. It seems as if Christ's death plays a relatively minor role.

JEHOVAH'S WITNESS: We believe that the human life Jesus laid down in sacrifice was equal to the human life Adam fell with. Since one man's sin caused all humans to be sinners, another man's sacrifice could balance the scales of justice.

CHRISTIAN: Okay, I think I've got a good grip on what Jehovah's Witnesses believe on all this. Can I now share with you what I believe the Bible teaches?

JEHOVAH'S WITNESS: Sure.

CHRISTIAN: As a Bible-believing Christian, I believe that salvation is 100 percent by God's grace. "Grace" literally means "unmerited favor." It refers to the undeserved, unearned favor of God. The word "unmerited" means this favor cannot be worked for. If grace is not free, it is not truly grace. What is your take on Romans 11:6, which says, "If it is by grace, it is no longer on the basis of works; otherwise grace would no longer be grace"?

JEHOVAH'S WITNESS: Well, we do believe in grace. We just believe grace gives us the opportunity to work out our salvation.

CHRISTIAN: Listen to Romans 11:6 again. "If it is by grace, it is no longer on the basis of works; otherwise grace would no longer be grace." This means that works can play no role in salvation. That's why Romans 6:23 tells us that "the free gift of God is eternal life in Christ Jesus our Lord." The words "free gift" mean we cannot earn eternal life. Titus 3:5 assures us that God "saved us, not because of works done by us in righteousness, but according to his own mercy."

JEHOVAH'S WITNESS: Do you think, then, that everybody is automatically saved since it is a free gift?

CHRISTIAN: That's a good question. Even though the gift is free, people have to receive the gift. If I hand you a gift, all you have to do is reach out your hands and receive it. We receive God's free gift of salvation by faith in Christ. This is what the apostle Paul taught in Ephesians 2:8-9. "For by grace you have been saved through faith. And this is not your own doing; it is the gift of God, not a result of works, so that no one may boast." So salvation is by grace through faith in Christ.

JEHOVAH'S WITNESS: You don't think good works pertain to salvation at all?

CHRISTIAN: [Smile.] Romans 3:20 instructs us, "For by works of the law no human being will be justified in his sight." In this context, the word "justified" means "acquitted of sin and declared righteous by God." Romans 3:20 says this cannot happen by good works. And Galatians 2:16 says, "A person is not justified by works of the law but through faith in Jesus Christ." God gives us salvation not on the basis of good works, but on the basis of faith in Christ. What do you think about these verses?

JEHOVAH'S WITNESS: I'm not quite sure. This is totally different from what I've been taught.

CHRISTIAN: Perhaps an illustration might help. The person who seeks salvation through self-effort is like the man who tried to sail across the Atlantic Ocean but found his sailboat becalmed for days with no wind. Finally, frustrated by his lack of progress, he tried to make his stalled sailboat move by pushing against the mast. Through strenuous effort, he made the boat rock back and forth and thereby created a few small waves on the otherwise smooth sea. Seeing the waves and feeling the rocking of the boat, he assumed he was making progress and continued his efforts. However, though he expended a lot of energy, he actually got nowhere.

This is essentially what it is like to try to obey the numerous rules of the Watchtower Society. You exert yourself a lot, but you actually get nowhere. Nobody is good enough to earn salvation by his works. That's why Christ died for you. He offers you the free gift of salvation by grace alone through faith alone. Christ alone is the one who can put salvation's winds into your sails.

JEHOVAH'S WITNESS: That's a good illustration.

CHRISTIAN: Did you know that some 200 times in the New Testament, salvation is said to be by faith alone? I could spend all day talking about this. But just to make my point, in John 3:15 Jesus said that all who believe in Him have eternal life. In John 11:25 He said that whoever believes in Him will live even though he dies. Doesn't that sound like good news?

JEHOVAH'S WITNESS: Hmm...

CHRISTIAN: Did you know that the word "gospel" literally means "good news"? The gospel is good news because salvation is entirely by God's grace and is received as a free gift through faith alone.

JEHOVAH'S WITNESS: "Faith alone" sounds too simple to me.

CHRISTIAN: Placing faith in Jesus Christ simply involves taking Him at His word. Faith involves believing that Christ is who He says He is. It also involves believing that Christ can do what He claimed He could do—He can forgive me and come into my life. Faith is an act of commitment in which I open the door of my heart to Him. We even see this in the New World Translation. In Acts 16:30-31 it reads, "And he [the jailer] brought them [Paul and Silas] outside and said: 'Sirs, what must I do to get saved?' They said: 'Believe on the Lord Jesus and you will get saved, you and your household.'"

JEHOVAH'S WITNESS: Well, that's interesting.

CHRISTIAN: I need for you to understand something very important before you leave today. Salvation is free, but it cost God everything to pay for it—that is, it cost Him the death of His very own

Son on the cross. Jesus's death for your sins didn't just take care of Adam's sin. It took care of your sins and my sins. As a result, if you trust in Jesus for salvation, God sees you as white as snow. Can I give you an illustration?

JEHOVAH'S WITNESS: Okay.

CHRISTIAN: If I look through a yellow glass, everything appears yellowish to me. If I look through a green glass, everything appears greenish. When God looks at the believer in Jesus Christ, God sees him through the white lens of Christ's perfect holiness. You've been washed clean. Because of Christ, you can be saved by grace alone through faith alone.

JEHOVAH'S WITNESS: That's another good illustration.

CHRISTIAN: Have you heard of the biblical concept of the kinsman-redeemer?

JEHOVAH'S WITNESS: No. What's that?

CHRISTIAN: In Old Testament times, a kinsman-redeemer was related to someone he was seeking to redeem from bondage. If someone was sold into slavery, for example, it was the duty of a blood relative—the next of kin—to act as that person's kinsman-redeemer and buy him out of slavery. Jesus is the Kinsman-Redeemer for sin-enslaved humanity. For Jesus to become a Kinsman-Redeemer, however, He had to become related by blood to the human race. That's why He, as God, became a man. Jesus, the God-man, is your Kinsman-Redeemer. Because Jesus is God, His blood had infinite value. This is one of the key teachings of the book of Hebrews.

JEHOVAH'S WITNESS: What you're saying doesn't seem compatible with Philippians 2:12, where we are told to work out our salvation with fear and trembling.

CHRISTIAN: I'm glad you brought up that verse. Would it surprise you to learn that many Christians believe this verse has nothing to do with the eternal salvation of individual believers?

JEHOVAH'S WITNESS: Yes it would.

CHRISTIAN: To understand this verse, we must keep in mind the state of affairs at the church in Philippi. This church had all kinds of problems. There were many rivalries among church members. Also, some Judaizers in the congregation were really rocking the boat, teaching church members that they had to get circumcised to be saved. The apostle Paul didn't like this at all. Because of these and other problems, Paul wrote them and told them to get their act together. He told them to work out their salvation on these issues. The Greek word for "work out" literally means "bring to a conclusion." Paul wanted them to bring all their internal problems to an end. Seen in that light, Philippians 2:12 has nothing to do with you trying to earn your salvation. Does that make sense to you?

JEHOVAH'S WITNESS: I've never heard it explained that way. Still, I can't get past the idea that God requires a life of good works.

CHRISTIAN: Well, let me comment on that. Bible-believing Christians believe that a life of good works and holiness is indeed important. But here's the important point: Good works follow salvation by grace alone, but good works don't cause that salvation. Works are not the condition of our salvation, but a consequence of it. We are saved by grace through faith—saved for good works. So don't get the cart before the horse. Salvation is by grace alone through faith alone. Once we've received that free gift, our motivation is to do good works in gratitude to God for what He's done for us. Does that put things into perspective for you?

JEHOVAH'S WITNESS: That is something to definitely think about.

CHRISTIAN: Here's what I think. I think you're a good person who is carrying a tremendous burden. It is the burden of a life of relentless good works inflicted on you by the Watchtower Society. They've told you that this will please Jehovah. In reality, Jehovah will rejoice when you receive the free gift of salvation in Jesus Christ. How about it? Would you like to receive that free gift today?

Conversation Highlights

Allow me to highlight a few tactical points from this conversation.

- My primary emphasis was salvation by grace through faith, but I also took aim at the Watchtower Society a few times.

- I corrected the works-understanding of Philippians 2:12, one of their primary verses.

- I quoted some of the very best verses in the New Testament on grace and faith.

- I used several illustrations to help clarify works versus grace.

- I closed the discussion by asking the Jehovah's Witness if he'd like to receive the free gift of salvation.

Digging Deeper

You may be interested in more in-depth information on the Jehovah's Witnesses' view of salvation and the specific Bible verses they cite to support it. If so, I invite you to consult my book *Reasoning from the Scriptures with the Jehovah's Witnesses* (2009 edition), pages 283–304.

Conversations About Soul Sleep and Hell

———

We have seen that the Watchtower Society teaches that there are two peoples of Jehovah with two very different destinies. The Anointed Class will be made up of 144,000 elite Jehovah's Witnesses who will dwell in heaven as spirit creatures and reign with Christ. The other sheep are all other Jehovah's Witnesses, who will live forever in an earthly paradise. This raises the question as to what happens to non-Jehovah's Witnesses. What does the future hold for the unsaved?

Jehovah's Witnesses believe there is no conscious existence of a person following the moment of death. In their thinking, there is no soul or spirit that is distinct from the human body that survives death. The word "soul" instead refers to the very life that a person has. Every human being is a combination of body and breath (Genesis 2:7) that together form a living soul. In view of this, Jehovah's Witnesses believe that all people have a soul in the sense that they have life.

The Watchtower view of the soul determines their view of what happens at death. Human beings do not have an immaterial nature that separates from the body at the moment of death. Rather, at death, the life force (soul) that is within them wanes and then ceases to exist.

This in turn determines their view of hell. Because human beings do not have an immaterial nature that survives death, they are obviously not conscious of anything following death. The Watchtower Society claims that "when a person is dead he is completely out of existence. He is not conscious of anything."[1] This is true of even righteous followers of Jehovah. They remain nonconscious until the future day of resurrection. For unbelievers, there is no suffering in flames of fire because there is no consciousness. Satan, the father of lies, is said to be behind the concept of eternal punishment in a flaming hell. The wicked cease to exist.

The Watchtower redefines hell as the common grave of all humankind. As such, both good and bad people are in this common grave following death. "Sheol and Hades refer not to a place of torment but to the common grave of all mankind."[2] Hell is "the common grave of dead mankind, the figurative location where most of mankind sleep in death."[3]

Falsehoods to Watch For

- Human beings do not have a separate immaterial nature known as the soul.
- The word "soul" refers to the life force within a person.
- At death, that life force wanes.
- There is no conscious existence following death.
- Hell is not a place of eternal suffering, but simply the common grave of humankind.

Important Points to Introduce

- The soul or spirit of a human being is an immaterial nature that consciously survives death.
- At death the soul or spirit departs from the body. Depending on whether one has trusted in Christ for salvation, the fully conscious soul goes to heaven or into eternal conscious punishment.
- Hell is a place of eternal conscious suffering.

Eavesdropping on a Conversation

JEHOVAH'S WITNESS: Good morning. Do you have a moment to chat? We're affiliated with the local Kingdom Hall.

CHRISTIAN: You're Jehovah's Witnesses, right? [Silently pray the open-the-heart prayer.]

JEHOVAH'S WITNESS: Right. Have you ever thought about what happens after death?

CHRISTIAN: Yes. I'm a Christian, and the Bible says a lot about the topic.

JEHOVAH'S WITNESS: Many Christian denominations have taught that at the moment of death, the soul of a person departs from the body and is still conscious.

CHRISTIAN: Well, yes, that's my view. The soul of the Christian goes to be with Christ in heaven, whereas the soul of the unbeliever goes to a place of punishment and holding, where he or she awaits the future great white throne judgment.

JEHOVAH'S WITNESS: We've learned that human beings do not have a soul or spirit that is distinct from the body. Rather, as Genesis 2:7 says, every person is a combination of the body and the breath that God gives that together forms a living soul. All people are souls in the sense that they have life.

CHRISTIAN: If that's so, then what do you think happens at the moment of death?

JEHOVAH'S WITNESS: Since we do not believe the Bible teaches that people have a separate immaterial nature, we do not believe they are conscious after death. At death, the life force in a person simply wanes. It fades. It ceases to exist.

CHRISTIAN: What do you think happens to God's followers at death? Do they lose all consciousness as well?

JEHOVAH'S WITNESS: Yes. They remain in a nonconscious state until the future day of resurrection. Once they are resurrected, their consciousness returns. Until then, they sleep in death.

CHRISTIAN: And the wicked?

JEHOVAH'S WITNESS: They are simply annihilated.

CHRISTIAN: So they don't suffer in hell?

JEHOVAH'S WITNESS: We believe that many Christian denominations have wrongly defined hell to be a place of fire and torment where the wicked suffer for all eternity. There is good reason to believe that hell is simply the common grave of humankind. Both good and bad people are in this common grave following death. The righteous will be resurrected. The wicked will not.

CHRISTIAN: Okay. I think I understand your view. You've mentioned the Bible several times. What specific verses can you cite that support your view?

JEHOVAH'S WITNESS: Genesis 2:7 in the New World Translation reads, "Jehovah God proceeded to form the man out of dust from the ground and to blow into his nostrils the breath of life, and the man came to be a living soul." Notice how this verse indicates that when God added breath to man's body, made of dust, man came to be a living soul.

CHRISTIAN: Is that the only verse?

JEHOVAH'S WITNESS: No, there are other verses as well. Consider Psalm 146:3-4. The New World Translation renders this passage, "Do not put your trust in nobles, nor in the son of earthling man, to whom no salvation belongs. His spirit goes out, he goes back to his ground; In that day his thoughts do perish." Ecclesiastes 9:5 in the New World Translation reads, "The living are conscious that they will die; but as for the dead, they are conscious of nothing at all." Such verses indicate that there is no conscious existence following the moment of death.

CHRISTIAN: Those are all interesting verses. I've actually done some study on all this. If you don't mind, I'd like to share with you what I believe to be a biblical view on all this. Would that be all right?

JEHOVAH'S WITNESS: Sure, I'm game.

CHRISTIAN: Good. First, from my studies, I've discovered that the word "soul" has a number of nuanced meanings in the Bible. Lots of words have different nuances of meaning in different contexts. I might illustrate what I'm talking about with the word "trunk." The word "trunk" can refer to the front of an elephant, the back of a car, a car, the bottom of a tree, the torso of a man, or a suitcase, depending on the context. Are you following me so far?

JEHOVAH'S WITNESS: Sure.

CHRISTIAN: Good. Likewise, the word "soul" has various meanings that depend on the context. For example, the word can refer to a living being, as Genesis 2:7 suggests. But simply because the word carries this meaning in that one verse does not mean that the word is limited to this one meaning. There are other verses that indicate other meanings for the word.

JEHOVAH'S WITNESS: Such as...

CHRISTIAN: Well, for example, the word can refer to a person's inner being, where he feels emotions. Deuteronomy 28:65 says a person's soul can be sad. Job 30:25 says a person's soul can be grieved. Genesis 42:21 says a person's soul can be distressed. So a person's soul can have emotional ups and downs. This is why the psalmist in Psalm 43:5 said, "Why are you cast down, O my soul, and why are you in turmoil within me?"

JEHOVAH'S WITNESS: Okay, but that still doesn't prove that man has a separate immaterial nature that can survive death.

CHRISTIAN: I'll grant you that. But I think other verses do support that meaning for the word "soul." For example, in Genesis 35:18 we read, "As her soul was departing (for she was dying), she called his name Ben-oni; but his father called him Benjamin." This verse seems to recognize the soul as distinct from the physical body, for at death the soul departs from the physical body.

JEHOVAH'S WITNESS: Hmm...I've not seen that verse before.

CHRISTIAN: Actually there are numerous biblical evidences that a person's immaterial nature, or soul, consciously survives death. Can I share some of these with you?

JEHOVAH'S WITNESS: I guess that would be okay.

CHRISTIAN: In Revelation 6:9-10 we read about some believers in God who were martyrs. They died for their faith. This passage indicates that their very souls were underneath God's altar and they are portrayed as talking to God. Their dead bodies were still on the earth, but their souls were in heaven talking to God. Doesn't that sound like the word "soul" refers to an immaterial nature in this context?

JEHOVAH'S WITNESS: Hmm…interesting.

CHRISTIAN: When Stephen was about to die as a result of being stoned, he looked up to heaven and said, "Lord Jesus, receive my spirit." That's in Acts 7:59. This must mean that the spirit survives death. This wouldn't make sense if we interpret the word "spirit" as the life force within Stephen that would cease to exist at the moment of death. Why would Stephen ask Jesus to receive something that was about to cease existing?

JEHOVAH'S WITNESS: Okay.

CHRISTIAN: Further, 1 Thessalonians 4:13-17 says that Christ will one day reunite the spirits or souls of His people in heaven with their resurrection bodies. While their spirits are with Christ in heaven, their bodies sleep on earth. Though the term "sleep" is often used to denote death in Scripture, it is never used in reference to a person's spirit or soul. The term "sleep" is always applied in Scripture to the body alone because in death the body takes on the appearance of one who is asleep. The most exciting part of 1 Thessalonians 4:13-17 is the statement that "God will bring with Jesus" all these spirits in heaven and reunite them with their resurrection bodies— bodies that have been sleeping in death on earth.

JEHOVAH'S WITNESS: I've never heard it explained that way before.

CHRISTIAN: There's another verse I want to share with you. In Philippians 1:21-23 the apostle Paul said, "For to me to live is Christ, and to die is gain. If I am to live in the flesh, that means fruitful labor for me. Yet which I shall choose I cannot tell. I am hard pressed between the two. My desire is to depart and be with Christ, for that is far better." How could Paul in his right mind refer to death as gain if death meant nonexistence?

JEHOVAH'S WITNESS: Hmm…good point.

CHRISTIAN: And Paul rejoiced that at the moment of death he would be with Christ in heaven.

JEHOVAH'S WITNESS: I noticed that.

CHRISTIAN: In a similar line of thought, Paul in 2 Corinthians 5:6-8 said, "So we are always of good courage. We know that while we are at home in the body we are away from the Lord, for we walk by faith, not by sight. Yes, we are of good courage, and we would rather be away from the body and at home with the Lord." Paul knew that the moment he died, his soul or spirit would be face-to-face with Christ in heaven. Doesn't that sound infinitely more appealing to you than the Watchtower position that you are not conscious following death?

JEHOVAH'S WITNESS: Well, I have to admit, I like that idea a lot more. The problem with your view, though, is that some verses indicate that people are not conscious following death. The passage I mentioned earlier, Psalm 146:3-4, is a good example. The New World Translation renders this passage, "Do not put your trust in nobles, nor in the son of earthling man, to whom no salvation belongs. His spirit goes out, he goes back to his ground; In that day his thoughts do perish." If his thoughts perish, that means he is unconscious.

CHRISTIAN: That's admittedly a difficult verse. I've always used a few interpretive principles to help me with difficult verses. One of these is that Scripture interprets Scripture. Another is this: Always interpret the difficult verses in light of what the clearer verses teach. The verses I shared with you a few moments ago clearly indicate conscious existence following death. That being the case, let's explore the meaning of Psalm 146:3-4.

JEHOVAH'S WITNESS: I'd be interested to hear your take on it.

CHRISTIAN: Many Bible scholars believe that when the psalmist said the dead person's "thoughts do perish," the word "thoughts" carries the nuance of plans, ambitions, and ideas for the future. In other words, a person's plans and ideas for the future die with him. So for example, when President Kennedy was assassinated back in the sixties, his plans and programs vanished with him. Does that make sense?

JEHOVAH'S WITNESS: I understand what you're saying. But what about Ecclesiastes 9:5? The New World Translation renders this verse,

"The living are conscious that they will die; but as for the dead, they are conscious of nothing at all."

CHRISTIAN: Well that's another great problem verse. Again, I believe that the clear verses of Scripture indicate that the soul does consciously survive death. We've seen this in 2 Corinthians 5:8, Philippians 1:21-23, and Revelation 6:9-10. We can look up those verses again if you like. In my thinking, we ought to interpret Ecclesiastes 9:5—a difficult verse—in light of what the clear verses teach. Does that make sense to you?

JEHOVAH'S WITNESS: I won't object.

CHRISTIAN: Many biblical scholars believe the verse means that the dead know nothing so far as their bodily senses and worldly affairs are concerned. But while they do not know what is happening on earth, they certainly do know what is going on in heaven, as we saw with the souls talking to God in Revelation 6:9.

JEHOVAH'S WITNESS: Okay, maybe.

CHRISTIAN: This brings me to make one more point. The Bible teaches that hell is, in fact, a place of conscious eternal punishment. Scripture uses a variety of words to describe the horrors of hell, including fire, fiery furnace, unquenchable fire, the lake of burning sulfur, the lake of fire, everlasting contempt, perdition, the place of weeping and gnashing of teeth, eternal punishment, darkness, the wrath to come, torments, damnation, exclusion, condemnation, retribution, woe, and the second death. The sobering thing is that the Bible indicates that the wicked who go there are in conscious torment.

Luke 16:22-28 indicates that the unsaved rich man who died was in conscious torment. Jesus Himself spoke repeatedly of the people in hell as consciously weeping and gnashing their teeth. An example is Matthew 8:12. This is a picture of perpetual conscious punishment. This leads me to a question. How can a wicked person suffer punishment if he is not conscious to experience that punishment?

JEHOVAH'S WITNESS: Hmm...I'm not sure about that.

CHRISTIAN: Wouldn't it seem silly for me to say, "I'm going to punish my car for not starting by slowly plucking out its sparkplugs one by one"? It would seem silly because my car is not conscious to receive that punishment.

JEHOVAH'S WITNESS: Ha. I see your point.

CHRISTIAN: In fact, wouldn't unconsciousness for the wicked ultimately be a gift or a blessing because it *avoids* punishment?

JEHOVAH'S WITNESS: Well, I've never thought of it that way.

CHRISTIAN: Scripture says God will hold the wicked accountable. At the great white throne judgment, He will assign different degrees of punishment depending on their level of wickedness. We see this in numerous Bible passages, including Matthew 11:21-24, Luke 12:47-48, John 15:22, Hebrews 10:29, and Revelation 20:11-15. I want to write down these passages so you can look them up later.

JEHOVAH'S WITNESS: Okay.

CHRISTIAN: The important thing is that Jesus died for our sins in order to make salvation possible. Those of us who trust in Him alone for salvation are exempt from any danger of hell. Jesus on the cross took what is ours (that is, our sin) so that He could give us what is His (that is, His eternal life). We might call this the great exchange. The salvation I'm talking about is by grace alone through faith alone. There's nothing we can do to earn it. Salvation is a free gift. Can we spend our remaining time together talking about this wondrous gift of salvation? I'd also like to tell you how Jesus changed my life forever. (See chapter 19, "Conversations about Salvation.")

Conversation Highlights

Allow me to highlight a few tactical points from this conversation.

- I asked plenty of questions so the Jehovah's Witness could fully explain his position.
- I asked for specific biblical support for all doctrinal assertions.
- I tried to answer his objections to the idea of consciousness

in the afterlife, and I also presented a positive doctrinal exposition of the idea.

- I introduced several principles of Bible interpretation to help people deal with difficult Bible verses.

- I closed the discussion poised to share the gospel and my personal testimony.

Digging Deeper

You may be interested in more in-depth information on the Jehovah's Witnesses' view of hell and conscious eternal punishment and the specific Bible verses they cite to support it. If so, I invite you to consult my book *Reasoning from the Scriptures with the Jehovah's Witnesses* (2009 edition), pages 305–338.

Postscript:

A Challenge

My goal in this book has been to demonstrate how to engage in tactical conversations with Jehovah's Witnesses that will yield maximum evangelistic punch. The conversations I've demonstrated in the book are engineered to challenge the trustworthiness of the Watchtower Society and to help the Jehovah's Witness perceive the error of Watchtower theology—with gentleness and respect. The ultimate goal, of course, is that as we speak the truth in love, the Jehovah's Witness may become a believer in the true God, the true Savior Jesus Christ, and the true gospel that saves.

As we come to the end of our journey together, I want to briefly emphasize seven pointers as a challenge to each of us.

1. Always be willing to converse with Jehovah's Witnesses whenever they show up on the doorstep. As 1 Peter 3:15-16 puts it, you are to always be "prepared to make a defense to anyone who asks you for a reason for the hope that is in you; yet do it with gentleness and respect." The conversational approach demonstrated in this book shows you how to accomplish this.

2. We are "ambassadors for Christ, God making his appeal through us" (2 Corinthians 5:20). Ambassadors are always kind and respectful.

3. You and I are called to be the light of the world (Matthew 5:14). What does light do? One expositor explains it this way: "When we look into the biblical use of the term 'light,'

the central idea that emerges is that of clearly and attractively presenting God's truth to others, illuminating it in order to show it for what it really is…The distinctive idea seems to be that of lucidly articulating the content of the gospel message."[1] We can shine as lights in all our conversations.

4. God calls us to "contend for the faith that was once for all delivered to the saints" (Jude 3). The word translated "contend" was often used in New Testament times to refer to competition in athletic contests. The idea behind the word is that of an intense and vigorous struggle to defeat the opposition. You and I are to engage in vigorous conversations with Jehovah's Witnesses in order to defeat Watchtower error so that Jehovah's Witnesses might come to understand the gospel that saves.

5. Remember that you and I do not have the power in ourselves to convert anyone. That is God's job. You and I witness (Matthew 28:19-20; Acts 1:8); only our supernatural and miraculous God has the power to convert (see John 6:39-40,44).

6. Do not become discouraged if you do not see an immediate conversion after your dialogue with the Jehovah's Witness. Just focus on respectfully telling the truth and faithfully planting and/or watering the seed of the gospel. It is then in God's sovereign hands. As the Christian singer Keith Green once said, "Do your best, pray that it's blessed, and the Lord will take care of the rest."

7. If a Jehovah's Witness comes to see that you are right and decides to depart from the Watchtower, your job is not over. His Watchtower family members and friends will now no longer associate with him. You must therefore try to get him into a good church where he can be embraced by a new family of believers and grow in his understanding of biblical truth. Be there for him during this time of readjustment.

Let him know you are praying for him. Exchange phone numbers and email addresses so you can be a source of strength for him, especially for the initial three months following his conversion. Your compassion during this time will make all the difference.

May the Lord richly bless you as you continue to be a missionary on your own doorstep!

Bibliography

Primary Watchtower Publications

1975 Yearbook of Jehovah's Witnesses. Brooklyn: Watch Tower Bible and Tract Society, 1975.

Aid to Bible Understanding. Brooklyn: Watch Tower Bible and Tract Society, 1971.

Blood, Medicine and the Law of God. Brooklyn: Watch Tower Bible and Tract Society, 1961.

Creation. Brooklyn: Watch Tower Bible and Tract Society, 1927.

God's Kingdom of a Thousand Years Has Approached. Brooklyn: Watch Tower Bible and Tract Society, 1973.

Holy Spirit—the Force Behind the Coming New Order! Brooklyn: Watch Tower Bible and Tract Society, 1976.

Is This Life All There Is? Brooklyn: Watch Tower Bible and Tract Society, 1974.

Let God Be True. Brooklyn: Watch Tower Bible and Tract Society, 1946.

Let Your Name Be Sanctified. Brooklyn: Watch Tower Bible and Tract Society, 1961.

Life Everlasting in Freedom of the Sons of God. Brooklyn: Watch Tower Bible and Tract Society, 1966.

Light, vols. 1-2. Brooklyn: Watch Tower Bible and Tract Society, 1930.

Make Sure of All Things: Hold Fast to What Is Fine. Brooklyn: Watch Tower Bible and Tract Society, 1953.

Man's Salvation Out of World Distress at Hand! Brooklyn: Watch Tower Bible and Tract Society, 1975.

Millions Now Living Will Never Die. Brooklyn: Watch Tower Bible and Tract Society, 1920.

New World Translation. Brooklyn: Watch Tower Bible and Tract Society, 1981.

Paradise Restored to Mankind by Theocracy! Brooklyn: Watch Tower Bible and Tract Society, 1972.

Prophecy. Brooklyn: Watch Tower Bible and Tract Society, 1929.

Qualified to Be Ministers. Brooklyn: Watch Tower Bible and Tract Society, 1955.

Reasoning from the Scriptures. Brooklyn: Watch Tower Bible and Tract Society, 1989.

Reconciliation. Brooklyn: Watch Tower Bible and Tract Society, 1928.

Should You Believe in the Trinity? Brooklyn: Watch Tower Bible and Tract Society, 1989.

Studies in the Scriptures, vols. 1-7. Brooklyn: Watch Tower Bible and Tract Society, 1886-1917.

The Greatest Man Who Ever Lived. Brooklyn: Watch Tower Bible and Tract Society, 1991.

The Harp of God. Brooklyn: Watch Tower Bible and Tract Society, 1921.

The Kingdom Is at Hand. Brooklyn: Watch Tower Bible and Tract Society, 1944.

The Truth That Leads to Eternal Life. Brooklyn: Watch Tower Bible and Tract Society, 1968.

Theocratic Aid to Kingdom Publishers. Brooklyn: Watch Tower Bible and Tract Society, 1945.

Things in Which It Is Impossible for God to Lie. Brooklyn: Watch Tower Bible and Tract Society, 1965.

You Can Live Forever in Paradise on Earth. Brooklyn: Watch Tower Bible and Tract Society, 1982.

Your Will Be Done on Earth. Brooklyn: Watch Tower Bible and Tract Society, 1958.

Christian Books on the Jehovah's Witnesses

Ankerberg, John, and John Weldon. *The Facts on Jehovah's Witnesses*. Eugene: Harvest House, 1988.

Bodine, Jerry, and Marian Bodine. *Witnessing to the Witnesses*. Irvine: Christ for the Cults, 1972.

Bowman, Robert M. *Jehovah's Witnesses, Jesus Christ, and the Gospel of John*. Grand Rapids: Baker Books, 1989.

Bowman, Robert M. *Understanding Jehovah's Witnesses*. Grand Rapids: Baker Books, 1991.

Bowman, Robert M. *Why You Should Believe in the Trinity*. Grand Rapids: Baker Books, 1989.

Chretien, Leonard, and Marjorie Chretien. *Witnesses of Jehovah*. Eugene: Harvest House, 1988.

Countess, Robert H. *The Jehovah's Witnesses' New Testament*. Phillipsburg: Presbyterian and Reformed, 1982.

Geisler, Norman, and Ron Rhodes. *Correcting the Cults*. Grand Rapids: Baker Books, 2004.

Grieshaber, Erich, and Jean Grieshaber. *Exposé of Jehovah's Witnesses*. Tyler: Jean Books, 1982.

Grieshaber, Erich and Jean Grieshaber. *Redi-Answers on Jehovah's Witnesses Doctrine*. Tyler: Jean Books, 1979.

Gross, Edmond. *We Left Jehovah's Witnesses*. Nutley: Presbyterian and Reformed, 1974.

Hoekema, Anthony A. *The Four Major Cults*. Grand Rapids: Eerdmans, 1978.

Lingle, Wilbur. *20 Important Questions for Jehovah's Witnesses*. Fort Washington: CLC, 1997.

Lingle, Wilbur. *Approaching Jehovah's Witnesses in Love: How to Witness Effectively Without Arguing*. Fort Washington: CLC, 2007.

MacGregor, Lorri. *Coping with the Cults*. Eugene: Harvest House, 1992.

MacGregor, Lorri. *What You Need to Know About Jehovah's Witnesses*. Eugene: Harvest House, 1992.

Magnani, Duane. *The Watchtower Files*. Minneapolis: Bethany House, 1985.

Martin, Walter, and Norman Klann. *Jehovah of the Watchtower*. Minneapolis: Bethany House, 1974.

Martin, Walter. *The Kingdom of the Cults*. Minneapolis: Bethany House, 1982.

Reed, David. *How to Rescue Your Loved One from the Watch Tower*. Grand Rapids: Baker Books, 1989.

Reed, David. *Index of Watchtower Errors*. Grand Rapids: Baker Books, 1990.

Reed, David. *Jehovah's Witnesses Answered Verse by Verse*. Grand Rapids: Baker Books, 1992.

Rhodes, Ron. *The 10 Most Important Things You Can Say to a Jehovah's Witness*. Eugene: Harvest House, 2001.

Rhodes, Ron. *The Challenge of the Cults and New Religions*. Grand Rapids: Zondervan, 2001.

Rhodes, Ron. *Find It Quick Handbook on Cults and New Religions*. Eugene: Harvest House, 2005.

Rhodes, Ron. *Jehovah's Witnesses: What You Need to Know*. Eugene: Harvest House, 1997.

Rhodes, Ron. *Reasoning from the Scriptures with the Jehovah's Witnesses*. Eugene: Harvest House, 2009.

Sire, James W. *Scripture Twisting: 20 Ways the Cults Misread the Bible*. Downers Grove: InterVarsity, 1980.

Thomas, F.W. *Masters of Deception*. Grand Rapids: Baker Books, 1983.

Tucker, Ruth. *Another Gospel*. Grand Rapids: Zondervan, 1989.

Weathers, Paul G. "Answering the Arguments of Jehovah's Witnesses Against the Trinity," in *Contend for the Faith*. ed. Eric Pement. Chicago: EMNR, 1992.

Books on Effective Conversation

Downs, Tim. *Finding Common Ground*. Chicago: Moody, 1999.

Geisler, Norman, and David Geisler. *Conversational Evangelism: How to Listen and Speak So You Can Be Heard*. Eugene: Harvest House, 2009.

Hybels, Bill, and Mark Mittelberg. *Becoming a Contagious Christian*. Grand Rapids: Zondervan, 1994.

Koukl, Gregory. *Tactics: A Game Plan for Discussing Your Christian Convictions*. Grand Rapids: Zondervan, 2009.

Newman, Randy. *Corner Conversations: Engaging Dialogues about God and Life*. Grand Rapids: Kregel, 2006.

Newman, Randy. *Questioning Evangelism: Engaging Peoples' Hearts the Way Jesus Did*. Grand Rapids: Kregel, 2004.

Rainer, Thom. *The Unexpected Journey: Conversations with People Who Turned from Other Beliefs to Jesus*. Grand Rapids: Zondervan, 2005.

Sherrard, Michael. *Relational Apologetics*. Brooks: Hill Harow Books, 2012.

Reference Books

Archer, Gleason. *Encyclopedia of Bible Difficulties*. Grand Rapids: Zondervan, 1982.

Arndt, William, and Wilbur Gingrich. *A Greek-English Lexicon of the New Testament and Other Early Christian Literature*. Chicago: University of Chicago, 1957.

Brown, Colin, ed. *New International Dictionary of New Testament Theology*. Grand Rapids: Zondervan, 1979.

Brown, Francis, S.R. Driver, and Charles A. Briggs. *A Hebrew and English Lexicon of the Old Testament*. Oxford: Clarendon, 1980.

Douglas, J.D., ed. *New Bible Dictionary*. Wheaton: Tyndale House, 1982.

Geisler, Norman, and Thomas Howe. *When Critics Ask*. Wheaton: Victor, 1992.

Harris, R. Laird, ed. *Theological Wordbook of the Old Testament*. Chicago: Moody, 1981.

Smith, Jerome H., ed. *New Treasury of Scripture Knowledge*. Nashville: Thomas Nelson, 1992.

Tenney, Merrill C., ed. *Zondervan Pictorial Encyclopedia of the Bible*. Grand Rapids: Zondervan, 1978.

Thayer, J.H. *A Greek-English Lexicon of the New Testament*. Grand Rapids: Zondervan, 1963.

Vine, W.E., Merrill F. Unger, and William White, eds. *Vine's Expository Dictionary of Biblical Words*. Nashville: Thomas Nelson, 1985.

Zodhiates, Spiros. *The Complete Word Study Dictionary*. Chattanooga: AMG, 1992.

Notes

Introduction: Why Another Book on Jehovah's Witnesses?

1. Kathi Hudson, *Raising Kids God's Way* (Wheaton: Crossway, 1995), p. 14.

2. Thomas Constable, Notes on 1 Thessalonians. See notes on 5:20-21. Available online at sonic light.com/constable/notes/pdf/1thessalonians.pdf.

3. Adrian Rogers, *Believe in Miracles but Trust in Jesus* (Wheaton: Crossway, 1997), p. 15.

4. Cited in Charles Hodge, *Systematic Theology,* vol. 1, chapter 12, "Miracles" (Charleston: Nabu Press, 2010).

5. Henry Morris, *The Biblical Basis for Modern Science: The Revised and Updated Classic,* chapter 3, "Miracles and the Laws of Nature" (Green Forest: Master Books, 2002).

Chapter 1: Why Effective Conversation Matters

1. Cited by Jason Barker, "Christians and Interreligious Dialogue," Watchman Fellowship. Available online at www.watchman.org/articles/other-religious-topics/christians-and-interre ligious-dialogue/.

2. Wilbur Lingle, *Approaching Jehovah's Witnesses in Love* (Fort Washington: CLC, 2007), p. 26.

3. Lingle, p. 20.

4. David R. Walls and Max Anders, *1, 2 Peter, 1, 2, & 3 John, Jude,* vol. 11 of Holman New Testament Commentary, ed. Max Anders (Nashville: B&H, 1999), p. 54.

5. John Phillips, *Exploring the Epistles of Peter: An Expository Commentary* (Grand Rapids: Kregel Academic, 2005), p. 153.

6. Walls and Anders, p. 55.

7. Thomas Constable, Notes on 1 Peter. See notes on 3:15. Available online at soniclight.com/con stable/notes/pdf/1peter.pdf.

8. John MacArthur, *1 Peter,* vol. 26 of The MacArthur New Testament Commentaries (Chicago: Moody, 2004). See notes on 1:15.

9. Don Closson, "Tactics for an Ambassador," Probe Ministries. www.probe.org/site/c.fd KEIMNsEoG/b.6549811/k.730D/Tactics_for_an_Ambassador.htm.

10. Summarized by Closson, "Tactics for an Ambassador."

11. Kenneth L Barker, ed., *NIV Study Bible* (Grand Rapids: Zondervan, 1995). See notes on 1 Peter 3:15-16.

Chapter 2: The Importance of Listening

1. J. Alec Motyer, *The Message of James,* vol. 18 of The Bible Speaks Today New Testament Series (Downers Grove: IVP Academic, 1985), p. 65.

2. Donald W. Burdick, "James," in *Hebrews Through Revelation,* vol. 12 of Expositor's Bible Commentary, ed. Frank E. Gabelein (Grand Rapids: Zondervan, 1982). See notes on 1:19.

3. R.C. Sproul, ed., *Reformation Study Bible* (Phillipsburg: P&R, 2005). See notes on Proverbs 18:13.

4. Charles Strohmer, "Reaching Out to Unbelievers," *Christian Research Journal* 25, no. 1 (2002).

5. Michael Sherrard, *Relational Apologetics* (Brooks: Hill Harow, 2012), p. 58.

6. Norman Geisler and David Geisler, *Conversational Evangelism* (Eugene: Harvest House, 2009), p. 48.

7. Wilbur Lingle, *Approaching Jehovah's Witnesses in Love: How to Witness Effectively Without Arguing* (Fort Washington: CLC, 2007), p. 38.

8. Geisler and Geisler, p. 46.

9. Walter Martin, *The Kingdom of the Cults* (Minneapolis: Bethany House, 1999), p. 28.

Chapter 3: The Importance of Asking Questions

1. David Reed, *Jehovah's Witnesses: Answered Verse by Verse* (Grand Rapids: Baker, 1992), p. 115.

2. Michael Sherrard, *Relational Apologetics* (Brooks: Hill Harow, 2012), p. 67.

3. Norman Geisler and David Geisler, *Conversational Evangelism* (Eugene: Harvest House, 2009), p. 26.

4. Gregory Koukl, *Tactics: A Game Plan for Discussing Your Christian Convictions* (Grand Rapids: Zondervan, 2009), p. 47.

5. Koukl, p. 49.

6. Don Closson, "Tactics for an Ambassador," Probe Ministries. Available online at www.probe.org/site/c.fdKEIMNsEoG/b.6549811/k.730D/Tactics_for_an_Ambassador.htm.

7. Koukl, p. 59.

8. Koukl, p. 88.

9. "Do You Know the Truth?" April 1, 1999. Cited in John Ankerberg and John Weldon, *Fast Facts on Jehovah's Witnesses* (Eugene: Harvest House, 2003), p. 154.

10. *The Watchtower,* December 1, 1998, pp. 17-18; cited in Wilbur Lingle, *20 Important Questions for Jehovah's Witnesses* (Fort Washington: CLC, 1997).

Chapter 4: The Importance of Effective Redirection

1. See my book *Reasoning from the Scriptures with the Jehovah's Witnesses* (Eugene: Harvest House, 2009), pp. 393-97.

2. Norman Geisler and David Geisler, *Conversational Evangelism* (Eugene: Harvest House, 2009), p. 106.

3. This is different from dealing with atheists, who do not believe in God, Jesus, or salvation. Finding common ground with atheists is more difficult.

Chapter 5: The Importance of Avoiding Offense

1. Charles Strohmer, "Reaching Out to Unbelievers," *Christian Research Journal* 25, no. 1 (2002).

2. *The ESV Study Bible* (Wheaton: Crossway, 2008). See notes on Proverbs 12:18.

3. John F. Walvoord and Roy B. Zuck, eds., *The Bible Knowledge Commentary: Old Testament* (Wheaton: Victor, 1985). See notes on Proverbs 15:1.

4. *The Bible Knowledge Commentary.* See notes on Proverbs 25:15.

5. D.A. Garrett, Proverbs, *Ecclesiastes, Song of Songs,* vol. 14 of The New American Commentary, ed. E. Ray Clendenen (Nashville: B&H, 1993), p. 207.

6. Thomas Constable, Notes on James. See notes on James 3:5-6. Available online at www.sonic light.com/constable/notes/pdf/james.pdf.

7. Strohmer, "Reaching Out to Unbelievers."

Chapter 6: The Importance of Speech Peppered by Grace

1. Curtis Vaughan, "Colossians," in *Ephesians Through Philemon,* vol. 11 of *The Expositor's Bible Commentary,* ed. by Frank E. Gaebelein (Grand Rapids: Zondervan, 1978). See notes on Colossians 4:5-6.

2. Thomas Constable, Notes on the Colossians. See notes on Colossians 4:6. Available online at www.soniclight.com/constable/notes/pdf/colossians.pdf.

3. *The ESV Study Bible* (Wheaton: Crossway, 2008). See notes on Colossians 4:5-6.

4. *Ryrie Study Bible* (Chicago: Moody, 2012). See notes on Colossians 4:5-6.

5. Adam Pelser, "Becoming a 'Seasoned' Apologist," *Christian Research Journal* 31, no. 1 (2008).

6. Wilbur Lingle, *Approaching Jehovah's Witnesses in Love* (Fort Washington: CLC, 2007), p. 23.

7. Walter Martin, "The Do's and Don'ts of Witnessing to Cultists," *Christian Research Newsletter,* January–February 1992, p. 4.

8. David Reed, *Jehovah's Witnesses Answered Verse by Verse* (Grand Rapids: Baker, 1992), pp. 115-16.

Chapter 7: The Importance of Your Testimony

1. Wilbur Lingle, *Approaching Jehovah's Witnesses in Love* (Fort Washington: CLC, 2007), pp. 43-44.

Chapter 8: Conversations About the Watchtower Society

1. Cited in Leonard and Marjorie Chretien, *Witnesses of Jehovah* (Eugene: Harvest House, 1988), p. 33.

2. *The Watchtower,* March 1, 1983, p. 25.

3. *The Watchtower,* March 15, 1969, p. 172.

4. *The Watchtower,* December 1, 1981, p. 27.

5. *The Watchtower,* July 1, 1973, p. 402

6. *The Watchtower,* April 1, 1919, reprints, p. 6414.

7. *The Watchtower,* July 1, 1973, p. 402.

8. *The Watchtower,* June 1, 1985, p. 19.

9. *The Watchtower,* May 1, 1957, p. 274.

10. *The Watchtower,* January 15, 1983, p. 22.

Chapter 9: Conversations About the New World Translation

1. *The Watchtower,* January 1, 1993, 19b; see also *Jehovah's Witnesses: The Organization Behind the Name,* video produced by The Watch Tower Bible and Tract Society (Brooklyn, 1990).

2. Raymond Franz, *Crisis of Conscience* (Atlanta: Commentary Press, 1983), p. 50, footnote 15.

3. Walter Martin, *The Kingdom of the Cults* (Minneapolis: Bethany House, 2010), p. 124.

4. You are welcome to download helpful documentation at my website, ronrhodes.org. Click on the tab "Odds and Ends." Then click on "Resources for Conversations with Jehovah's Witnesses."

Chapter 10: Conversations About Jehovah

1. *Let Your Name Be Sanctified* (Brooklyn: Watch Tower Bible and Tract Society, 1961), p. 88.
2. *The Watchtower,* March 15, 1975, p. 174.
3. *The Watchtower,* May 15, 1969, p. 307.
4. *The Watchtower,* December 15, 1984, p. 29.
5. You are welcome to download helpful documentation at my website, ronrhodes.org. Click on the tab "Odds and Ends." Then click on "Resources for Conversations with Jehovah's Witnesses."

Chapter 11: Conversations About Jesus and the Archangel Michael

1. *Aid to Bible Understanding* (Brooklyn: Watch Tower Bible and Tract Society, 1971), p. 1152.
2. *Reasoning from the Scriptures* (Brooklyn: Watch Tower Bible and Tract Society, 1989), p. 218.
3. *The Watchtower,* December 15, 1984, p. 29.
4. Available at my website, ronrhodes.org. Click on the tab "Odds and Ends." Then click on "Resources for Conversations with Jehovah's Witnesses."

Chapter 12: Conversations About Jesus and Jehovah

1. *The Watchtower,* November 1, 1964, p. 671.
2. *Awake!,* November 8, 1972, p. 28.
3. *You Can Live Forever in Paradise on Earth* (Brooklyn: Watch Tower Bible and Tract Society, 1982), p. 143.
4. Aid to Bible Understanding (Brooklyn: Watch Tower Bible and Tract Society, 1971), p. 1395.
5. Available at my website, ronrhodes.org. Click on the tab "Odds and Ends." Then click on "Resources for Conversations with Jehovah's Witnesses."

Chapter 13: Conversations About Jesus's Crucifixion

1. *Awake!,* September 22, 1974, p. 28.
2. *Awake!,* November 8, 1972, p. 28.
3. *The Watchtower,* August 15, 1987, p. 29.
4. *Reasoning from the Scriptures* (Brooklyn: Watch Tower Bible and Tract Society, 1989), p. 89.
5. *Reasoning from the Scriptures,* p. 89.
6. *The Watchtower,* May 1, 1989, p. 23.
7. Available at my website, ronrhodes.org. Click on the tab "Odds and Ends." Then click on "Resources for Conversations with Jehovah's Witnesses."

Chapter 14: Conversations About Jesus's Resurrection

1. *Studies in the Scriptures,* vol. 7 (Brooklyn: Watch Tower Bible and Tract Society, 1917), p. 57.
2. *Let Your Name Be Sanctified* (Brooklyn: Watch Tower Bible and Tract Society, 1961), p. 266.
3. *Aid to Bible Understanding* (Brooklyn: Watch Tower Bible and Tract Society, 1971), p. 1395.
4. *You Can Live Forever in Paradise on Earth* (Brooklyn: Watch Tower Bible and Tract Society, 1982), p. 145.

5. *The Watchtower,* September 1, 1953, p. 518.

6. *Things in Which It Is Impossible for God to Lie* (Brooklyn: Watch Tower Bible and Tract Society, 1965), p. 354.

7. *Aid to Bible Understanding,* p. 141.

8. *The Greatest Man Who Ever Lived* (Brooklyn: Watch Tower Bible and Tract Society, 1991), chapter 131.

9. Available at my website, ronrhodes.org. Click on the tab "Odds and Ends." Then click on "Resources for Conversations with Jehovah's Witnesses."

Chapter 15: Conversations About Jesus's Second Coming

1. *Studies in the Scriptures* (Brooklyn: Watch Tower Bible and Tract Society, 1886-1917), pp. 2:239, 3:234.

2. *Studies in the Scriptures,* vol. 4, p. 621.

3. *Studies in the Scriptures,* vol. 7, p. 386.

4. *Let God Be True* (Brooklyn: Watch Tower Bible and Tract Society, 1946), p. 250.

5. *The Watchtower,* January 15, 1993, p. 5.

6. *What is Truth?* (Brooklyn: Watch Tower Bible and Tract Society, 1932), p. 48.

7. *Studies in the Scriptures,* vol. 3, p. 126.

Chapter 16: Conversations About the Holy Spirit

1. *Reasoning from the Scriptures* (Brooklyn: Watch Tower Bible and Tract Society, 1989), p. 381.

2. *Should You Believe in the Trinity?* (Brooklyn: Watch Tower Bible and Tract Society, 1989), p. 20.

3. *The Watchtower,* July 1, 1973, p. 402.

4. *Aid to Bible Understanding* (Brooklyn: Watch Tower Bible and Tract Society, 1971), p. 781.

5. Available at my website, ronrhodes.org. Click on the tab "Odds and Ends." Then click on "Resources for Conversations with Jehovah's Witnesses."

Chapter 17: Conversations About the Trinity

1. *The Watchtower,* April 1, 1970, p. 210.

2. *Studies in the Scriptures,* vol. 5 (Brooklyn: Watch Tower Bible and Tract Society, 1899), p. 76.

3. *Let God Be True* (Brooklyn: Watch Tower Bible and Tract Society, 1946), p. 102.

4. *Reconciliation* (Brooklyn: Watch Tower Bible and Tract Society, 1928), p. 101.

5. *Examining the Scriptures Daily* (Brooklyn: Watch Tower Bible and Tract Society, 2012). See the entry for Friday, January 25.

6. *What Does the Bible Really Teach?* (Brooklyn: Watch Tower Bible and Tract Society, 2005), p. 202.

7. *Studies in the Scriptures,* vol. 5 (Brooklyn: Watch Tower Bible and Tract Society, 1899), pp. 60-61; see also Let God Be True, p. 100.

Chapter 18: Conversations About the Anointed Class and Other Sheep

1. *Reasoning from the Scriptures* (Brooklyn: Watch Tower Bible and Tract Society, 1989), p. 76.

2. *The Watchtower,* February 1, 1982, p. 28, insert added; see also The Watchtower, December 15, 1982, p. 19.

3. *Reasoning from the Scriptures,* p. 79.

Chapter 19: Conversations About Salvation

1. *The Watchtower,* August 15, 1972, p. 491.

2. *Reasoning from the Scriptures* (Brooklyn: Watch Tower Bible and Tract Society, 1989), p. 308.

3. *Reasoning from the Scriptures,* p. 308.

4. Duane Magnani, *The Watchtower Files* (Minneapolis: Bethany House, 1985), p. 232.

Chapter 20: Conversations About Soul Sleep and Hell

1. *You Can Live Forever in Paradise on Earth* (Brooklyn: Watch Tower Bible and Tract Society, 1982), p. 88.

2. *You Can Live Forever in Paradise on Earth,* p. 83; see also *Reasoning from the Scriptures* (Brooklyn: Watch Tower Bible and Tract Society, 1989), pp. 168-75.

3. "What Are Sheol and Hades?" Watchtower Online Library, Watch Tower Bible and Tract Society, 2013. Available online at wol.jw.org/en/wol/d/r1/lp-e/1102005157?q=what+are+sheol+and+hades&p=par.

Postscript: A Challenge

1. Bill Hybels and Mark Mittelberg, *Becoming a Contagious Christian* (Grand Rapids: Zondervan, 2008), p. 45.

Other Great Harvest House Books by Ron Rhodes

Books About the Bible

- The Big Book of Bible Answers
- Bite-Size Bible® Answers
- Bite-Size Bible® Charts
- Bite-Size Bible® Definitions
- Bite-Size Bible® Handbook
- Commonly Misunderstood Bible Verses
- The Complete Guide to Bible Translations
- Find It Fast in the Bible
- The Popular Dictionary of Bible Prophecy
- Understanding the Bible from A to Z
- What Does the Bible Say About…?

Books About the End Times

- 40 Days Through Revelation
- Cyber Meltdown
- The End Times in Chronological Order
- Northern Storm Rising
- Unmasking the Antichrist

Books About Other Important Topics

- 5-Minute Apologetics for Today
- 1001 Unforgettable Quotes About God, Faith, and the Bible
- Angels Among Us
- Answering the Objections of Atheists, Agnostics, and Skeptics
- Christianity According to the Bible
- The Complete Guide to Christian Denominations
- Find It Quick Handbook on Cults and New Religions
- The Truth Behind Ghosts, Mediums, and Psychic Phenomena
- What Happens After Life?
- Why Do Bad Things Happen If God Is Good?
- The Wonder of Heaven

The 10 Most Important Things Series

- The 10 Most Important Things You Can Say to a Catholic
- The 10 Most Important Things You Can Say to a Jehovah's Witness
- The 10 Most Important Things You Can Say to a Mason
- The 10 Most Important Things You Can Say to a Mormon
- The 10 Things You Need to Know About Islam
- The 10 Things You Should Know About the Creation vs. Evolution Debate

Quick Reference Guides

- Halloween: What You Need to Know
- Islam: What You Need to Know
- Jehovah's Witnesses: What You Need to Know

The Reasoning from the Scriptures Series

- Reasoning from the Scriptures with Catholics
- Reasoning from the Scriptures with the Jehovah's Witnesses
- Reasoning from the Scriptures with Masons
- Reasoning from the Scriptures with the Mormons
- Reasoning from the Scriptures with Muslims

Little Books

- The Little Book About God
- The Little Book About Heaven
- The Little Book About the Bible

To learn more about Harvest House books and
to read sample chapters, visit our website:

www.harvesthousepublishers.com

HARVEST HOUSE PUBLISHERS
EUGENE, OREGON